Cathedrals of
Britain

Cathedrals of Britain

North of England and Scotland

Bernadette Fallon

First published in Great Britain in 2017 by
Pen & Sword History
an imprint of
Pen & Sword Books Ltd
47 Church Street
Barnsley
South Yorkshire
S70 2AS

ISBN 978 1 52670 384 2

A CIP catalogue record for this book is available from the British
Library

Typeset in Ehrhardt by
Mac Style Ltd, Bridlington, East Yorkshire
Printed and bound in the UK by CPI Group (UK) Ltd,
Croydon, CR0 4YY

Pen & Sword Books Ltd incorporates the imprints of Pen & Sword
Archaeology, Atlas, Aviation, Battleground, Discovery, Family
History, History, Maritime, Military, Naval, Politics, Railways,
Select, Transport, True Crime, Fiction, Frontline Books, Leo
Cooper, Praetorian Press, Seaforth Publishing and Wharncliffe.

For a complete list of Pen & Sword titles please contact
PEN & SWORD BOOKS LIMITED
47 Church Street, Barnsley, South Yorkshire, S70 2AS, England
E-mail: enquiries@pen-and-sword.co.uk
Website: www.pen-and-sword.co.uk

Contents

Acknowledgements

Thank you to everybody who so generously gave their time, expertise and support to this book:

Catherine Hodgson, Ruth Rubson, David Farrell-Banks and Gina Davis at Durham Cathedral; Sarah Johnson, Katherine Capocci, and Yvonne Wilkinson at Visit Durham; Godfrey Wilson and Julia Barker at Ripon Cathedral; Tracy Morgan at Visit Harrogate; Neil Holland, Richard York, Karn Dyson and Malcolm Warburton at Wakefield Cathedral; Marie Christopher at Welcome to Yorkshire; Emma Gittins, Nigel James and Nicola Burgin at Sheffield Cathedral; Wendy Ulyett at Marketing Sheffield; Sandra Heaton, Jon Howard and Gillian Davies at Bradford Cathedral; Patricia Tillotson at Bradford Tourism; Kirsty Mitchell, Tom Outing, Stacey Healey, Sharon Atkinson at York Minster; Kay Hyde at Visit York; Stephen Preston and Sarah O'Connor at St Giles' Cathedral Edinburgh; Delaine Kennedy at St Machar's Cathedral, Aberdeen; Evelina Andrews and Rebecca Lowe at Visit England; Erin Hickey and Michael McCuish at Visit Scotland.

Introduction

Power, glory, bloodshed, prayer: cathedrals in the UK are as much about human drama as spiritual sanctuary, as much about political wrangling as religious fervour. From Christian beginnings in the Middle Ages through Reformation, Renaissance and Modernity, the great cathedrals of Britain have been both battleground and place of quiet reflection, created for the glory of God for sure, but also for the glory of men.

Cathedrals are the link to our Medieval past, a living, breathing connection to a part of our ancient history, a continuous thread through centuries of change. But the story of these sacred sites stretches back even further. Many of today's cathedrals are built on prehistoric places of worship, from Roman temples to early Pagan shrines. And many of today's religious customs and celebrations also have their origin in a Pagan past. So Samhain, the festival of the dead, re-emerges as All Souls Day in the Christian calendar, while the midwinter solstice is now known as Christmas.

A cathedral takes its name from the word 'cathedra', which means the seat or throne of a bishop. A cathedral is a church where a bishop sits. While we don't know much about the origin of cathedrals or early Christianity in Britain, Christian vessels from the 3rd century have been uncovered in Cambridgeshire, as well as a Christian cemetery dating from the same time in Dorset. In Iron Age England, it was believed that the cockerel was a defence against thunderstorms, and so the cockerel has evolved to its place on church steeples, as a weathercock.

We know that the Roman Empire adopted Christianity following Constantine's conversion in 312, after he was proclaimed emperor in York in 306. Records from this period show that three English bishops – from York, Lincoln and London – travelled to an ecclesiastical council in Arles, southern France. It's safe to assume they travelled from their respective cathedrals, though no traces of these early cathedrals remain. For very good reason. It's likely that today's cathedrals were built on the same site as their distant predecessors, a living contemporary link with an ancient past.

The Roman Empire was in decline from the end of the 4th century, and the subsequent Saxon invasions destroyed the formal Christian church. In the 6th century, several Celtic missionaries are credited with restoring Christianity to Scotland and the north of England, in what was then known as the Kingdom of Northumbria. This region stretched from Edinburgh and Lothian right down to the Humber, incorporating the counties of Durham and York and the holy isle of Lindisfarne. But it is to an island further than this that we look to for the rise of Christianity in the region.

The Irish saint Columba was an abbot and missionary who studied under Ireland's most prominent church figures and founded several monasteries in his native country. But after an argument that led to a bloody battle, Columba was sent into exile. He was tasked with saving as many souls through his preaching as had been lost in the fighting.

In 563 he came to the island of Iona on the west coast of Scotland. It is said that this was the first piece of land from which he could no longer see his native Ireland and so was allowed to settle there. He founded an abbey on Iona that became an important religious and political institution in the region for centuries afterwards, and also a centre for literacy and learning. He went on to found several churches in the Hebrides and launch the legend of the Lough Ness monster. The story was that he banished a ferocious 'water beast' to the depths of the lake after it killed and attacked several of his disciples.

One of the students who came to be educated on Iona was Oswald of Northumbria, later St Oswald, who was raised as a king in exile. He wanted to restore Christianity to his people and, on taking the crown of Northumbria in 634, requested that missionaries be sent from Iona to spread the faith. After one unsuccessful attempt where the attending bishop claimed the Northumbrians were too stubborn to be converted, a second missionary was sent. This was Aidan, who came to be known as the Apostle of Northumbria.

Aidan was a disciple of Columba and an Irish monk from the monastery on Iona. He founded a monastic cathedral on Lindisfarne, an island that is still a place of pilgrimage and retreat today. As Bishop of Lindisfarne, he constantly travelled throughout the country spreading the gospel and was responsible for the construction of churches, monasteries and schools across Northumbria. He died in 651 and his body is buried under the abbey at Lindisfarne. He is recognised as a saint by the Roman Catholic, the Anglican and the Orthodox churches.

The Celtic missions proved so successful that Northumbria became one of the leading areas of Christianity in the country, alongside Kent. Kent had been converted by Augustine, a Benedictine monk and the prior of a monastery in Rome, sent by Pope Gregory in 597 to lead what has become known as the Gregorian mission in Britain. Augustine became the first Archbishop of Canterbury and is considered to be the Apostle to the English and a founder of the English church.

To this day, the church in England continues to be led from the cathedrals of Canterbury in Kent and York in what was formerly Northumbria. The pope's influence in Canterbury meant this area followed the Church of Rome's calendar, while Northumbria followed the Celtic Christian tradition. However, the two regions aligned to follow the Roman calendar and its calculation of Easter after the 664 Synod of Whitby. We'll find out more about this in later chapters.

That we know so much about this period and its personalities is thanks to one man, Bede, also known as the Venerable Bede, who wrote the *Ecclesiastical History of the English People*, a history of the church in England that was completed around 731. It's thought he was born near Durham and entered a monastery at a young age, devoting the rest of his life to scholarly learning and writing. He was ordained a deacon, then a priest, and was canonised a saint after his death.

He wrote about the early Celtic Christian saints – Columba, Aidan and Oswald – and also the famous northern saints – Wilfrid, Cuthbert, Chad, Hilda, John of Beverley, and Etheldreda. Some scholars suggest that he didn't actually like Wilfrid very much.

We've already heard about Columba, Aidan and Oswald. In the coming chapters, we'll meet Wilfrid, Cuthbert, Chad, Hilda, John of Beverley, Etheldreda and Bede himself. Wilfrid was responsible for creating what is today the oldest surviving Saxon crypt in the country. Without Cuthbert there would be no cathedral in Durham. Hilda and Etheldreda are two strong and powerful women of the Middle Ages, both of whom shaped the path of Christianity in Britain.

The Middle Ages saw an unprecedented rise in the building of cathedrals and churches that would later become cathedrals. All over Europe, countries were covered with castles and churches. But even before the coming of William the Conqueror in 1066, and the new skills and building knowledge this brought, we know that several mighty cathedrals were already in place.

Many towns grew out of the expansion of churches, monasteries and minsters during this period. But churches were not used solely for sacred purposes. Records from the time show them being used as meeting places, markets and even occasionally alehouses. Priests were not necessarily devout men of prayer. Unlike their counterparts in abbeys and monasteries, many were illiterate, many were married and many were reported for violence and drunkenness. They were as experienced in Pagan customs as Christian rituals, and many practised magic in the community.

William the Conqueror introduced many reforms, and also Norman clergy to bring new order to the church structure and religious communities. He appointed a new Archbishop of Canterbury, an Italian called Lanfranc, who drew up the first principles of canon law, set up ecclesiastical courts to address spiritual matters and decreed that clergy should not be allowed to marry. It was now that the great cathedrals began to rise. In fact, York Minster grew as a direct challenge to Lanfranc's rule, as we will see.

Building these huge cathedrals was a mammoth task in the Middle Ages, even with the skills of the Norman stonemasons. Whole armies of builders were needed for construction and the only power was manpower, with animals working alongside. Stones had to be transported from quarries to cathedral sites. A huge variety of skills was needed on the site, from stonecutters and masons, carpenters, roofers, painters and glaziers, down to the unskilled work of diggers and labourers. Master Masons devised and supervised the work.

Many workers followed the building projects around the country and across Europe, though there was a difference in building in France and England as England's boat-building experience was put to use in its native cathedrals. For this reason you'll find many wooden ceilings and ornate wooden carvings throughout the country, and a cathedral ceiling is often said to resemble the upturned hull of a ship. In fact, the English word for the cathedral's central aisle, the nave, comes from the Latin word 'navis', which also gives us the word 'navy'.

Cathedrals were places of community. People attended services regularly and the rite of worship marked out the important events in their lives, their births, marriages and deaths, alongside everyday acts of penance, thanksgiving, prayers of intercession and prayers for the dead. Traditionally, a cathedral's layout from west to east traces the journey of life from birth to death, with the baptismal font located inside the west door.

The people came to visit relics, the bones and body parts of important saints, that were the source of much of the church's wealth, as pilgrims paid to see them. They came to marvel at the cathedral's treasures, to be awed by the majesty of the building and to receive a religious education.

Services were lively affairs. The clergy were separated from the congregation by the rood screen dividing the quire and sanctuary, the private area, from the public space of the nave. But this was a community get-together, a social event as much as a spiritual one. Stories were swapped, gossip was shared, the hum of conversation was often loud as the mass took place behind the screen. The cathedral hosted public meetings, and famous visiting preachers, chapters and councils met there. Markets were sometimes held in the nave.

We know that early cathedrals were not colourless inside, and were not the buildings of plain stone we know today. Small traces reveal them to be richly styled and lavishly decorated, covered in bright colours and gilding. Ornate wooden carvings were given full expression in spaces like the quire, with their eye-catching misericords. These 'mercy seats' were installed for the comfort of the clergy, who had to stand up for very long periods during prayers. A ledge under the tip-up seat provided a place to them to perch for comfort and support.

As the population swelled in the Middle Ages, so too did the congregations. Chantry chapels vied for space in the aisles, set up by wealthy patrons who paid priests to say masses for departed family members. Believing the purchase of prayers smoothed the soul's journey to heaven from purgatory, the sale of masses became big business for the church. York Minster had as many as sixty chantry chapels at the height of their popularity.

Religion was becoming commodified, the wealthy could 'buy' their way into heaven. Churches were objectified, with their statues, relics, icons and other treasures a way of attracting people to the building for money. The church was rich and powerful, the biggest landowner in the country and also the largest employer. Bishops and abbots lived in a state of luxury and even the lowlier monks lived comfortably. Gambling and drinking were not uncommon.

Growing objections to the direction the church was taking was one of the main driving forces behind the Reformation and the renouncing of the Catholic faith, although today we mainly associate it with King Henry VIII's desire to divorce his first wife, Catherine of Aragon, so he could marry Anne Boleyn.

The pope wouldn't give him a divorce so Henry cast out the pope and set up the reformed church, with himself at the head. Monasteries and abbeys were dissolved, churches were plundered for their treasures and lands. As the old church was seen to be riddled with idol-worship and controlled by the clergy for material gain, the new church was set up to be austere, prayerful and closer to God. And to grant Henry his divorce.

But the disgruntled rumblings against the old forms of worship had been growing for many centuries. Monarchs wanted the church's wealth, worshippers disagreed with its doctrines. In the 13th century, King John, with his eye on the money, rejected the pope's nominee for the position of Archbishop of Canterbury, was duly excommunicated and happily took possession of the church's revenues for a while before being accepted back into the papal fold.

The 14th-century Lollards launched a major revolt against the Catholic church with the translation of the Bible into English, bringing the word of God closer to the people, without need for clerical translation or intervention. They claimed the sacraments were dead signs and there was no purgatory, so masses for the dead were pointless. Matters finally came to a head in the 16th century, when King Henry VIII invoked the 1534 Acts of Supremacy that established the Church of England.

Scotland too split from the Catholic church and the Scottish parliament rejected the mass and papal jurisdiction in 1560. John Knox was one of the leaders of the Scottish Reformation, a vocal spokesperson against Catholicism whose beliefs had forced him into imprisonment and exile. We'll meet him again in a later chapter.

Nobody knows how much was lost during the destruction wrecked by the Reformation, as sacred objects, relics, artworks, books and manuscripts were destroyed or defaced. But for all that has been lost, much has been gained over the centuries and the stories of the cathedrals' evolution are the stories of the communities that surround them.

Holy shrines have always told the stories of their communities, from the mighty stone buildings we visit today to the barrow graves and holy wells of prehistoric times. Simple stone crosses once marked the places where many magnificent cathedrals now stand. Cathedrals provide a continuous link to the living past, they bring the Middle Ages to life in the 21st century. They are places of worship and prayer for sure but also, just as they were back then, they are places to stand and stare and marvel.

Let us take you on a marvellous journey…

Chapter 1

York

Spiritual centre in the north of England: York Minster

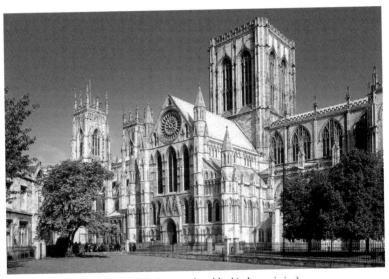

York Minster. (© *Chapter of York: reproduced by kind permission*)

York Minster is one of the biggest Medieval Gothic cathedrals in northern Europe and holds half of all the Medieval stained-glass in England. As the Mother Church of the Northern Province, it's one of Britain's most important spiritual centres and the seat not only of a bishop but an archbishop. It costs £20,000 a day to run and employs a full-time staff of 200, including thirty permanent glaziers and stonemasons, as well as 500 volunteers.

Its history stretches back to the Roman Emperor Constantine, who founded the first church in York in the 4th century. The first minster was a wooden church built in 627 for the baptism of King Edwin of Northumbria. Although the current minster is an impressive 800 years old, dating back to the 13th century when the 250-year building programme began, this is in fact the fourth minster to be built in the city – three others predate it.

What's the difference between a cathedral and a minster?

Traditionally a minster is the Anglo-Saxon name for a missionary church and a minster was a church that had its own clergy or a church attached to a monastery. The word is associated with the Latin *monasterium* or monastery. Today it's an honorific title given to particular churches in England. A cathedral is the seat of a bishop and the word is derived from the chair he sits on – the 'cathedra' – which makes York Minster both a minster and a cathedral. And its full name reflects this, 'The Cathedral and Metropolitical Church of St Peter in York'.

Emperor Constantius I died in 306 AD and his son Constantine was proclaimed emperor as he visited the Roman troops stationed in York. He built York's first place of worship to celebrate the news. The remains of the basilica he created can still be seen today beneath the minster in the undercroft, a fascinating link to the building's early history.

The first York Minster was built in Saxon times by King Edwin, inspired – or in fact, instructed – by a woman. Edwin wanted to marry Ethelburga of Kent. She would only agree to come to York if she could continue her Christian worship. And along with Bishop Paulinus, one of the pope's missionaries, she ended up converting Edwin to Christianity too. Built for his baptism in 627, the first church was a small wooden structure that was eventually rebuilt in stone.

Due to King Edwin's efforts and Paulinus' success in bringing Christianity to the people, York became an important religious and spiritual centre. In 735, when Pope Gregory III appointed Egbert as the first Archbishop of York, York Minster became the most important church in northern England, a status it retains to this day.

Edwin's stone church burned down in 741 and was replaced just in time for the Viking invasion – the first recorded attacks took place in 866. But it appears that the Vikings respected York's symbolic importance and, in 895, King Guthfrith, a Christian Viking, was buried in the minster.

The building was in a sorry state by the time William the Conqueror invaded England in 1066. He installed Thomas of Bayeux as Archbishop of York and in 1080 started to construct a new building in the Romanesque, or Norman, style. Not only was it the biggest church, it was also the biggest building in the north of England and dominated the landscape for miles around.

It was, in fact, a very pointed message from Thomas to his rival Lanfranc, the Archbishop of Canterbury. Lanfranc had already claimed primacy for Canterbury over York. By building a minster to rival the size of Canterbury Cathedral, Thomas was in effect thumbing his nose at the opposition. Work was completed on his 'message' around 1100.

But this still isn't the church we see today. York Minster is one of the finest examples of Gothic architecture in England and the new-style building gradually replaced the older Romanesque design over a period of more than 200 years. The first phase of rebuilding started around 1215 under Archbishop Walter de Gray and continued under twenty more archbishops, finally completing in 1472. Small 'shadows' still exist, however. We know that the former Norman cathedral was the width of today's nave pillars, for example.

The nave was one of the earliest parts of the cathedral to be developed, between 1291 and 1350, in the ornately decorated Gothic style, with pointed rather than rounded arches allowing it to take greater weights and achieve soaring heights. It's the widest Gothic nave in England and also one of the longest.

The history of the West Window

The majestic West Window sits over the great west doors, the ceremonial entrance to the minster leading to the mighty nave. Eight of York's archbishops range along the bottom of the glass, including Archbishop Melton, who commissioned it in 1338. Above are the twelve apostles, though fitting all twelve into the eight horizontal panes means that some of them have had to double-up. Next come four pairs of panels depicting the life of Christ and the Blessed Virgin, from Annunciation to Nativity, Resurrection and Ascension. Above it all is a scene set in heaven, showing Mary crowned as queen sitting beside Christ. The beautiful heart shape of the stone tracery at the top gives the window the name it's locally known by, 'the heart of Yorkshire'.

But be aware that you're looking at a mix of the 1330s and the 1980s when you gaze at this historic relic. The stonework of the frame had to be completely replaced in 1989 due to the effects of pollution and erosion, and the external carved arches of the doorway below were replaced in 1998.

Curious facts: the headless saints

Between the window and the doorway, the headless 'semaphore' saints raise their flags. If you know your semaphore history, you'll realise that 'flag semaphores' – a system of sending messages by holding flags in certain positions according to an alphabetic code – were not widely used until the 19th century. A long time after the 1300s.

In fact, the saints are only ten years old. They were put on temporary exhibition in the cathedral and proved so popular with visitors that the church authorities bought them. But what are they signalling with their flags and why are they headless? Their flags spell out the phrase 'Christ is here'. Their headless status we'll come to later.

Don't miss: body parts in the bosses

There are aspects of both mystery and humour in the nave. Although it dates from the Medieval period, the roof with its bosses doesn't. It was destroyed by fire in 1840 and the current ceiling and all of its decorations are Victorian. The Victorians faithfully copied the designs of the Medieval bosses – all except one. Seven are exact replicas of representation of scenes from the life of Christ. The eighth, representing the Nativity, shows Mary feeding the baby Jesus from a bottle, Victorian sensibilities being too delicate to show her breastfeeding as she had been in the Medieval design. Look out also for Christ's ascension into heaven – a very literal representation, accurately represented by the soles of his feet!

The famous dragon's head is located halfway up the nave on the north side. It's a solid oak carving, but its purpose remains a mystery. There's a chain through the dragon's neck. What was it used for? There's a lot of speculation but the most commonly accepted theory is that it's the remains of a very elaborate lifting mechanism. Maybe it was used to raise the 50-foot-high cover on the Medieval font that was lost during the time of the Reformation.

That's not all that was lost in the Reformation. The aforementioned heads came a cropper also. Around the church you'll see them, full-bodied representations of saints and religious icons, cut off at the neck. The 'semaphore' angels over the door are headless in sympathy with them, though they were created 500 years later.

The Reformation was not the only scourge faced by York Minster. It has also been plagued by fire, and three major fires have caused severe damage throughout its history.

The Nave. (© *Chapter of York: reproduced by kind permission*)

The quire, traditionally where services are sung and where the Archbishop of York has his cathedra, has a surprisingly modern feel. Instead of Medieval misericords, York Minster quire has fixed seats. The woodwork seems fresher, less faded. This is because all of the original woodwork, the roof and some of the stonework of the quire were destroyed by fire in 1829.

It was started by Jonathan Martin who had written several warning letters to the minster clergy complaining about how the church was being run. As his letters were ignored he decided to take matters into his own hands and stayed behind one night after evensong to set the blaze. The quire was completely destroyed. He was found guilty but not of sound mind and was sent to the Criminal Lunatic Department of Bethlem Hospital where he died nine years later.

The tower burned down in 1840 when a workman making repairs accidentally left a candle burning. The tower was timber, as was the roof of the nave, which was also destroyed. You can still see evidence of the 19th-century flames around the nave's stone pillars, where several are coloured pink.

Curious facts: the illusion of the windows

Today's tower is the same size as its Norman predecessor and you can have some fun with perspective here. Ask anybody to judge which windows are bigger – the windows high above in the tower or the Five Sisters Window in the north transept. To the eye, the Five Sisters Window looks the taller of the two. But it's an optical illusion, created by the angle of the tower. They are in fact all the same size.

The south transept features the famous Rose Window. Its stonework dates from 1240 and the glass from the early 1500s, representing the Lancaster and Tudor roses. The window marked the union of the Houses of York and Lancaster under Henry VII. It is also sometimes known as the Marigold Window, due to the shape of its tracery.

Rose Window. (© *Chapter of York: reproduced by kind permission*)

Which brings us to the third fire, a much more recent occurrence in 1984, when a lightning storm hit the roof of the south transept, causing it to erupt in flames. Firemen trained water on it to make it cave-in and to prevent the flames spreading to the rest of the building. Afterwards there were 40,000 cracks in the Rose Window and it's estimated if the heat of the fire had been two degrees higher, the lead holding it together would have melted and it would have been destroyed. Today the window is sandwiched between two panes of clear glass for protection.

Don't miss: the 'Blue Peter' bosses

But out of the ashes rose the phoenix. After the devastation of the south transept, work began to rebuild the roof and all of its bosses. Iconic children's TV show *Blue Peter* got involved and children all over the UK were invited to design bosses for inclusion in the new ceiling. Out of 34,000 entries, six were selected to be featured and provide interesting cultural references to what was uppermost in the mind of a child at that time.

Here you'll see the man on the moon and Neil Armstrong, famine relief and save the whale. While the words 'raising the Mary Rose' might not ring many bells today, in the early 1980s it was a topic much discussed as a team of divers, archaeologists and scientists recovered the Tudor warship from the sea bed off the Isle of Wight. The excavation recovered thousands of artefacts from the time of King Henry VIII, ironically the man who was responsible for so much of the demolition of York Minster. The winning entry features a white and red rose surrounded by flames, a symbol of the beauty that grew out of destruction.

The south transept is the oldest part of the building and its construction began in 1220, largely the work of Archbishop de Gray. An enormously wealthy man, rumour has it that he paid £10,000 of his own money to the pope and Catholic clergy of the time to secure his position. Luckily he had enough money left over to start work on the cathedral building.

Opposite the Rose Window in the north transept, the Five Sisters Window is more austere in its tall grandeur and very much darker. It dates from a similar time, built in the mid-1200s, but why so different? A number of reasons in fact. The window is filled with grisaille glass. The word grisaille comes from the French for 'greyness'. Don't forget that while the structure of the Rose Window was created in the early 1200s, the colourful glass dates from the 16th century. And because the glass is older in the Five Sisters, it's had to have a lot more repairs. Back in the day, that meant using lead to fill in cracks, blocking the light even further.

But there is something very contemporary about this window and that is its geometric patterning, reminiscent of Islamic design. It is said the window was commissioned by five unmarried sisters who

Five Sisters Window. (© *Chapter of York: reproduced by kind permission*)

were keen embroiderers and enjoyed working on patterns. Charles
Dickens' *Nicholas Nickleby* features the legend of how the Five
Sisters Window was created.

Don't miss: the Chapter House

The minster's Chapter House is an architecture jewel in a building that shines brightly with them. It was built between 1260 and 1286 in the Decorated Gothic style and is a work of complex engineering as it doesn't have a central column to support its huge vaulted ceiling. There's a model of the roof in the vestibule entrance showing the huge complexity of its architecture.

It's an important historical space in its own right, as well as part of the minster. Soon after its completion at the end of the 13th century, it was used for the assembly of parliaments by Edward I and Edward II during their campaigns against the Scots. And it's still used as a meeting place for certain parliaments, the College of Canons, who use it for assemblies, as well as for part of the installation of new canons.

Around the walls are the forty-four seats of the college and it is here you will find the minster's finest carvings, from the macabre to the comical. There are reflections on the people of York – watch out for the hairstyles and hats in particular. There are birds of prey

Chapter meeting in Chapter House. (© *Chapter of York: reproduced by kind permission*)

pecking out human eyes, there are cats advancing on mice. There are over 2,000 carvings in total, in both wood and stone, and every single one has a distinctive feature about it.

Curious facts: horses in the cathedral

It's lucky we still have the Chapter House to admire at all. During the Civil War it fell into disuse and it was decided to sell it, stone by stone, to a local businessman who planned to use the stones to build a stable. He died before work could begin, however, and the Chapter House remained intact. It's not the only association the building has with horses. One of the chapels off the north side of the nave, St Sepulchre's Chapel, was used as a stable for horses before it was demolished in 1816.

Don't miss: the minster's chapels

There were sixty chapels in the minster before the Reformation. Today there are just fifteen. The oldest one is located in the south transept, the Chapel of St Michael and All Angels, and was established by the famous Archbishop de Gray in 1241.

It was the original site of his tomb after his death, but today you'll find this in the transept, an elaborate construction of Purbeck marble and limestone with a large ornate canopy. Around the building you'll find memorials in all shapes and styles, from the brightly painted almost cartoon-like memorial to Sir William Ingram and his wife, to the bare cadaver of Thomas Haxey, a 15th-century minster treasurer, stripped of clothing and in a state of decay.

Don't miss: the Great East Window

One thing that certainly isn't bare or – thanks to recent substantial renovations – in a state of decay is the cathedral's crowning stained-glass-glory, the Great East Window. This was the work of John Thornton of Coventry in the 15th century, the foremost master glazier of his day. We know it took him three years to complete – from 1405 to 1408 – and we know he was paid £56 for it, including a £10 bonus for finishing on time. It seems like a bargain. Its 21st-century restoration is costing £10 million and each pane of glass takes two to three months to be restored.

This is one of the finest and largest Medieval stained-glass windows in the world and is bigger than a tennis court. It contains 117 panels in rows of nine and a tracery at the top. It tells generation upon generation of stories, from the seven days of Creation to a foretelling of the end of the world in a graphic representation of the Book of Revelation.

Curious facts: two times a bishop

It features saints including St Cuthbert and St William, the latter having the unusual honour of being made Archbishop of York twice in his lifetime. Falling out of favour during his first incarnation he was removed by the pope from his position. But once his enemies disappeared, his followers petitioned his return. A huge throng turned out to welcome him back to the city, with so many crowding onto the bridge over the River Ouse that it collapsed and they all tumbled into the water below. Miraculously nobody drowned in the accident and William was subsequently canonised a saint after his death.

There are two other things to do before you leave York Minster. One involves travelling up to the heavens, the other descending to the depths. You can climb to the top of the tower for an additional entrance fee, though be warned that the several hundred steps follow a narrow and steep winding path. The views from the top over York and surrounding countryside are worth it, though. It's an easier journey down to the undercroft to see the history of the entire building come together in a fascinating space that exposes the building's Roman, Norman and Gothic architecture, buried deep below the minster.

Visiting York Minster

Guided tours take place regularly throughout the day. For more information and opening times visit Yorkminster.org.

York: where to go and what to do

York is England's most visited city outside London and as soon as you arrive, you'll see why. This beautiful Medieval city with its stunning culture and history is a magnificent historical record of the past, with its narrow winding streets enclosed by 13th-century walls and, at its heart, the awe-inspiring minster. After you've visited the cathedral, however, you'll find there's a wealth of other attractions – historical and contemporary – to entertain you.

York began life as a Roman garrison, used by Hadrian as the base for his northern campaign. From the Romans, the town passed into the hands of the Anglo-Saxons and several centuries later it became the Viking capital in Britain for a hundred years. Norman rule after 1066 established the magnificent minster and the city became an important trading and religious centre. Interestingly, it's the Vikings who made the biggest mark if we count this as the naming of the city – the name 'York' is derived from its Viking name 'Jorvik'.

The city is well-served by rail and bus connections, but driving can be problematic as Medieval towns were not designed with cars in mind. There are numerous park & ride car parks at the edge of the city, however, and it's very easy to get around central York on foot, with all of the major sites within easy access.

To steep yourself completely in York's Medieval history and enjoy close links with the cathedral's past, check into Gray's Court Hotel in Chapter House Street, just a short cobbled-street's walk from the minister, tucked into a hidden courtyard that makes it feel like a real find. And what a find it is.

Part of it dates back to 1080, commissioned by the first Norman Archbishop of York to provide the official residence for the treasurers of the minster. The last of the treasurers resigned in 1547, when the house was surrendered to the crown during the Reformation. Its first new owner was the Duke of Somerset, who was given the house by King Edward VI, the son of King Henry VIII. It has been a luxury boutique hotel since the early part of the 21st century, is possibly the oldest continuously occupied house in the UK and it retains the only private access to York's city walls, which surround the edge of its lovely gardens.

An excellent place to start your tour of York – after the magnificent minster of course – is the Jorvik Viking Centre, where you can retrace its fascinating Viking past. The centre brings the former Viking settlement to life – right down to supplying the smells – through a 'time capsule' rail journey that takes you through 9th-century 'Jorvik'.

Take a step back even further in time by walking the city walls, which follow the line of the original Roman walls. The full circuit is 4½ miles, so allow a couple of hours for the journey – and wear comfortable shoes. A good place to start is the Museum Gardens or at Bootham Bar, which is on the site of a Roman gate. Bear in mind when visiting York that 'gate' here means street and 'bar' means gate – which should avoid any confusion when following directions or looking at street signs.

Monk Bar is the best-preserved Medieval gate in the city. Here you'll also find the Richard III Museum that investigates the mystery of the princes in the tower who may or may not have been murdered by their uncle, King Richard. And continue your excavations of Roman history in the Yorkshire Museum, which takes you back to the pre-Jorvik days when the city was known as 'Eboracum', with maps and models of the Roman city. There are also exhibits on Viking and Medieval York.

York was a very fashionable place to be seen in during the 1800s, attracting lots of the aristocracy. And it became a very busy hub in 1839 with the arrival of the railway, as you'll discover on a trip to the excellent National Railway Museum. It's one of the biggest railway museums in the world, packed full of exhibits including a replica of the world's first modern steam locomotive, George Stephenson's Rocket, and the Flying Scotsman, the first steam engine to break the 100mph barrier. You can even take the 'train' there. A road-train runs between the minster and museum throughout the day.

Art lovers can sate their desires at the York City Art Gallery, which has exhibited the likes of Joshua Reynolds and Paul Nash. Shoppers will find great browsing in the antique and bric-a-brac shops around the areas of Colliergate and Fossgate. There are a couple of good theatres in the city, though don't expect opera at the Opera House, it's a venue for live music and shows.

Chapter 2

Durham

Durham Cathedral: 'Half church of God, half castle 'gainst the Scot'

Durham Cathedral. (© *Durham Cathedral: reproduced by kind permission*)

Durham Cathedral was founded in 1093 when the Byzantine empire was in its heyday, the Nubian kingdom was at the peak of its power and Vikings were still roaming Europe. Today the Byzantines are gone and Vikings confined to fancy dress parties, but Durham Cathedral still stands and its soaring architecture remains, in the words of Sir Walter Scott, 'Half church of God, half castle 'gainst the Scot'.

Why Durham Cathedral marks a turning point in history

The design of Durham Cathedral not only pre-dates the Gothic architecture style that soared in popularity in the Middle Ages, it actually provided the inspiration for it. The Gothic style flourished in England from the 12th century until after the Renaissance, reviving again in the late 18th and throughout the 19th centuries. But it's here, in the otherwise Romanesque-styled Durham, we see the first use of ribbed high vaults.

Romanesque design is all about rounded arches – big, ponderous and heavy. Pointed arches look more refined, less weighty. They cut into the stonework so there's less wall space to deaden the eye. Instead, the pointed ribs draw the eye upwards making the roof they support look light and graceful rather than massive and solid. Drawing the eye upward gives the illusion of a building that is soaring into the sky towards God and reflecting his glory. The roof can also be seen for miles around, a solid testament in the landscape of the glory and power of God.

The pointed arches you see in the nave at Durham are hugely significant. They marked a turning point in the history of architecture, they led the way for a Gothic flourishing, most notable in the cathedrals of Canterbury and Westminster, but also in Salisbury, Lincoln and York. Most of the Durham vault has stood intact for 900 years, though some of the earliest sections of the wall collapsed and had to be rebuilt.

The carved pillars stretching the length of the nave are so wide that each one would take four people holding hands to circle them. They are 6.6 metres round and 6.6 metres high. The nave itself is 201 feet long and its vault is just under 73 feet high.

Power in the cathedral

Durham holds a key position in the Church of England hierarchy and the Bishop of Durham is the fourth most powerful seat in the church. Until the 19th century the bishop was a military leader as well as a religious one, known as 'prince bishop'.

Today the connections with royalty continue and the bishop stands at the right hand of the monarch at coronations. He doesn't live in the castle next door any more but you can still visit it. It is now part of Durham University and students give visitors guided tours. Along with the cathedral, the castle has also been designated a UNESCO World Heritage Site. It was in fact one of the first sites to be designated, around the same time as the Taj Mahal in India and the French Palace of Versailles.

William of St Carilef – William of Calais – was the first prince bishop and was appointed by William the Conqueror in 1080. He was responsible for getting the cathedral built and construction began in 1093 at the eastern end. First completed was the choir stalls and the builders moved on to the nave, which was fully completed almost forty years later.

The beautiful chapels you see around the cathedral were gradually added as the years went on, including the Chapel of the Nine Altars with its gorgeous stained-glass windows, including the beautiful Rose Window. The chapel was built between 1242 and 1280, so the many priests of the monastery each had place to say their daily masses.

Durham's beauty has been lauded by the literary greats. Writing of the cathedral in the late 1880s in *The English Notebooks*, Nathaniel Hawthorne said, 'I paused upon the bridge, and admired and wondered at the beauty and glory of this scene... it was grand, venerable, and sweet, all at once; I never saw so lovely and magnificent a scene, nor, being content with this, do I care to see a better.' And his fellow countryman and contemporary travel writer Bill Bryson gave Durham the 'vote for best cathedral on planet Earth' in *Notes from a Small Island*.

What you should know about Durham Cathedral

Cathedrals have for centuries been places of pilgrimage and prayer. And also of great competition as institutions vied with each other to attract the greatest numbers. Which is why Durham Cathedral is so important. Its key attraction, the relics of St Cuthbert, ensured pilgrims flocked to the city from all over the UK and beyond.

Who was St Cuthbert?

Cuthbert is the reason Durham Cathedral exists – and so no greater claim to his importance can be made. Born in Northumberland around 634, he was educated by Irish monks at Melrose Abbey on the Scottish borders and famed as a miracle worker during his lifetime.

He served as Bishop of Lindisfarne, a monastic community founded by St Aidan at the request of Oswald of Northumbria, from 685 to his death in 687. Around this time Lindisfarne was unfortunately rather popular with the Vikings and so to avoid the many plunders and thefts the monks fled from the area in 875, taking the bones of Cuthbert with them.

With nowhere safe to go, they continued to roam for almost a hundred years when, according to legend, they followed two milk maids who were searching for a brown (dun) cow. Once they reached a peninsula in the River Wear, Cuthbert's coffin could not be moved any further, the coffin had reached its apparent resting spot and the monks built a shrine to Cuthbert in that place.

From a simple temporary timber structure, the shrine became a church and, as Cuthbert's fame and reports of his miracles rose, it became a site of pilgrimage. Pilgrims brought money and Cuthbert brought royalty – the legendary King Canute of Denmark, England and Norway was an early pilgrim and granted land and recognition to the monastic community. And so the town of Durham and its cathedral began to grow.

St Cuthbert's shrine. (© *Durham Cathedral: reproduced by kind permission*)

A marble shrine was created for the relics, studded with jewels, ornaments and semi-precious stones. One monk's written account describes it as the most 'sumptuous in all England, so great were the offerings and jewells bestowed upon it, and endless the miracles that were wrought at it'.

Today a simple stone stab behind the high altar in the cathedral marks the resting place of St Cuthbert. The earlier elaborate monument was destroyed on the orders of Henry VIII during the Reformation. According to the six scrolls of the *Rites of Durham*, written in the mid-16th century about the cathedral and its traditions, Cuthbert's body was exhumed when the grave was plundered and discovered to be intact, with no signs of decomposition – 800 years after his death. An account, written much later, claims that the commissioners of Henry VIII sent to destroy his tomb, 'found him lying whole uncorrupt with his face bare, and his beard as of a fortnight's growth, and all the vestments about him as he was accustomed to say mass.'

Unfortunately, the monks didn't last as long and the monastery was dissolved on the final day of the year 1540. But some traces of their story remain. The street leading from the cathedral's east side, up to Palace Green, is named Dun (Brown) Cow Lane.

Cuthbert and the Venerable Bede

Which brings us to Bede, also known as the 'Venerable Bede', another one of Durham Cathedral's 'celebrities'. St Cuthbert was immortalised in history by Bede, whose remains are also kept here in the cathedral. As is the head of St Oswald of Northumbria.

Bede lived at the end of the 5th century and died in the 6th, was a monk from Northumbria and a scholar whose most famous work was the *Ecclesiastical History of the English People*. He wrote or translated around forty books in his lifetime and, quite incredibly, many of those books still survive today. Prolific to the last, he was still writing on his death bed and even composed a poem about his own death, which has the singular distinction of being the most widely copied poem in the Old English language. It's called *Bede's Death Song*.

Before the unavoidable journey there, no one becomes
wiser in thought than him who, by need,
ponders, before his going hence,
what good and evil within his soul,
after his day of death, will be judged.

Fore there neidfaerae naenig uuiurthit
thoncsnotturra than him tharf sie
to ymbhycggannae aer his hiniongae
huaet his gastae godaes aeththa yflaes
aefter deothdaege doemid uueorthae.

Bede's bones have been in the cathedral since the 11th century and were originally buried alongside Cuthbert's relics but now lie in the Galilee Chapel. Interesting place, the Galilee Chapel. One of the earlier additions to the cathedral, in the later part of the 12th century,

Bede's tomb. (© *Durham Cathedral: reproduced by kind permission*)

it was once the only part of the building that women could access. You can still see the black marble slab in the nave that marked their boundary. They had to stay behind this until the 16th century, when they were allowed to step over the threshold and into the main body of the building.

Curious facts: Harry Potter

An extra spire appeared on top of the famous Durham Cathedral tower in the 21st century – but only on film. Durham Cathedral is just one of the many famous buildings around the UK that have doubled as backdrops for the famous Hogwarts School of Witchcraft and Wizardry. So the tower was given a 'magic' spire and the cloisters also played their part as the magical snowy courtyard where Harry first releases Hedwig the owl in *Harry Potter and the Philosopher's Stone*. Less poetically, Ron does his slug vomiting here in *Harry Potter and the Chamber of Secrets*.

Curious facts: the unknown soldiers

In 2013, building work at the nearby Durham University's Palace Green Library uncovered two mass graves. At the time it was believed they might hold the bodies of Scottish soldiers, incarcerated in the cathedral as prisoners by Oliver Cromwell following the Battle of Dunbar in 1650. The battle left up to 5,000 dead and modern calculations suggest that an estimated 6,000 Scotsmen were taken prisoner. Three thousand were taken to Durham Cathedral but around 1,700 soldiers died in the march there. Nothing was ever known of the whereabouts of their bodies. Until now.

In 2015, the university announced that research on the remains of up to twenty-eight bodies established the skeletons were all male, aged between 13 and 25 years old and of likely Scottish origin. Radiocarbon dating analysis, as well as the fact that some of the prisoners had smoked clay pipes known to be in common use in Scotland after 1620, led to the establishment of the date of death as between 1625 and 1660. Experts say it is quite possible there are more mass graves under what are now university buildings. But for now, the mystery of what became of the poor souls who travelled from Scotland to Durham in their fight against the English has been solved.

Curious facts: the sanctuary knocker

The cathedral was a stark sanctuary for the prisoners, but back in Medieval times, any fugitive rapping the sanctuary knocker, which can still be seen on the cathedral's northern door, was given shelter and hidden for thirty-seven days. Wearing a black robe with St Cuthbert's cross sewn on the shoulder, given by the monks to identify the wearer as one who had been granted sanctuary by God and his saints, the fugitive was encouraged to reconcile with his enemies or plan his escape.

Don't miss: *Magna Carta*

Other than famous relics, pilgrimage attractions and a head, the cathedral holds an impressive collection of manuscripts dating from the 6th century, printed books from 1473, early local maps and prints and no less than three separate issues of *Magna Carta*, the cornerstone of the British constitution.

Don't miss: the fabulous view

One of the best 'treasures' of all is the view from the cathedral's mighty tower, open to visitors for a small admission price. It's an energetic climb, particularly near the top when the passageway narrows and the circular steps corkscrew steeply. You will be advised

Magna Carta. (© *Durham Cathedral: reproduced by kind permission*)

to leave any heavy bags in the care of staff at the foot of the tower – and will be very grateful for the advice several hundred steps up.

It's all worth it, though, stepping out on the tower's flat roof, the city streets and the hills and fields of north of England beyond them, surely one of the best views in all of all England. You may not see any university students among the admiring crowds on the rooftop, however. It is said to be unlucky for them to climb the tower before they graduate.

View from the tower. (© *Durham Cathedral: reproduced by kind permission*)

Don't miss: worship at the foot of Marks & Spencer

It is very inspiring to stand in the cathedral nave and consider the workmanship and know-how that went into creating this soaring structure. High above, windows stretch towards the heavens. It's not the original glass of course. The 16th-century Reformation plundering and destruction destroyed many original features, including the windows, in cathedrals right across the land.

The glass in the windows at Durham Cathedral dates mainly from the Victorian age. Apart from the glass in the window entitled 'Daily Bread', close to the main door. This has a much more recent provenance, 1984 to be exact. It was donated to the cathedral by the staff of Marks & Spencer in Durham, to mark the firm's centenary.

Marks & Spencer window. (© *Durham Cathedral: reproduced by kind permission*)

Visiting Durham Cathedral

Guided tours take place during the week or you can take a self-guided trail around the building, following the excellent printed material.

For more information on Durham Cathedral, including opening and service times, visit the website at Durhamcathedral.co.uk.

Durham: where to go and what to do

Out of the North Pennines, the stunning landscape of cathedral and castle rises to meet you on the Durham approach. Few towns have such an imposing aspect from such a distance. And the power of its beauty is in keeping with its historical power. Durham has been the seat of princes and bishops for centuries.

The cathedral is never far from your mind on the streets of Durham. Its Romanesque majesty rises above the hilly streets, though while the cathedral might dominate your visit, there are many other hidden gems in the area.

Not so hidden is Durham Castle, standing side-by-side with its religious neighbour. Built as a fort in 1072, it became the prince bishops' home until 1837 and now it's owned by Durham University. Even though it's a hall of residence, it's still possible to take a tour and you can even stay here if arranged in advance.

Outside the town, the Beamish Open-air Museum is a working museum that allows you to step back in time to the 19th and 20th centuries and see what life was like for industrial workers who weren't lucky enough to be princes or bishops. The last mine closed here in 1984, during challenging and difficult times for mine-workers and their families. Here you can visit a working farm, take a trip underground into the mines and visit recreations of a school, dentist and pub from the time. Tour the pit cottages and don't leave without taking a ride behind an 1815 Steam Elephant locomotive or a replica of Stephenson's famous Locomotion No 1.

Explore the area's historical past in the Durham Museum & Heritage centre, close to the cathedral. Here you'll find the origins of the Medieval town, ruled over by the prince bishops from their castle, ever watchful against the constant raids of the Scots. Here too you'll find information on the city's powerful families, including the Nevilles of Brancepeth and Raby, who produced several kings, among them Edward IV, Edward V and Richard III.

You can explore the outdoors in the city's Botanic Gardens, 10 hectares of garden set among mature woodlands on the southern outskirts of the city. Or take a trip down the Wear on a river cruise and enjoy the city's majestic landscape from another aspect.

On the banks of the river, watch out for the ruins of Finchale Priory, now managed by the National Trust. The abbey was founded in 1196 on the site of the hermitage of St Godric, who was a retired sailor and merchant. It's thought that he devoted himself to Christianity after a visit to Lindisfarne Priory on Holy Island. It functioned as an outpost of Durham Cathedral and, in fact, hosted the monks on their holidays until the time of the Reformation, when so many abbeys and monasteries were destroyed. Remains of the original church of St Godric still stand, as well as his tomb.

And if you've had enough of history by now, there's always Diggerland, with Durham's 'rides and drives' where you can have a go at driving everything from a mini Land Rover to a JCB.

Durham's visitor centre is located in the 19th-century almshouse World Heritage Site in the city and open seven days.

Durham has a very good train service, connecting the city with Scotland and the rest of the UK. Trains to Edinburgh, London, Newcastle and York are frequent. It's also served by national and local buses.

Chapter 3

Ripon

Ripon Cathedral: from the 7th to the 21st century

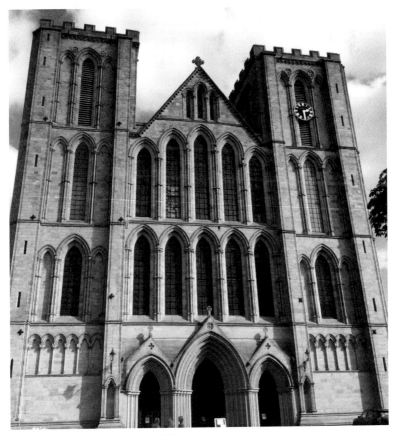

Ripon Cathedral. (© *Bernadette Fallon*)

Ripon cathedral may hold the body of one of the greatest early saints of England and might just have provided the inspiration for one of the best-known books in the English language. But we do know this for sure. While this is not the oldest church building in the UK, the 7th-century crypt at Ripon dates from 672 and predates every existing cathedral in the country. For this we have St Wilfrid to thank.

Wilfrid was a learned and religious man, an abbot, a bishop of several dioceses, and canonised a saint after his death. He was also a global traveller and adventurer, a frequent visitor to Rome and the pope and, by all accounts, a very colourful character, whose quarrels with kings led to exile and imprisonment. Not that this deterred him. His exile from one part of the country led to his establishment of monasteries and churches in another, and he is credited with spreading the word of Christianity to many Pagan settlements. This doesn't mean he led an austere life. Apparently, he went to France to organise his own consecration as Bishop of York by twelve other bishops, which took about three years.

Artist Sally Scott has created a contemporary memorial of his life in glass close to the entrance of today's cathedral. He's flanked by angels in the centre panel to symbolise his spiritual journey. His earthly journeys are represented by his pilgrimages to Rome and Sussex – where it's rumoured he taught them how to fish – and France – where it's rumoured he was in big demand as a husband for local daughters.

Curious facts: the timing of Easter

Wilfrid is also one of the reasons that we celebrate Easter when we do. He acted as spokesman for introducing the Roman calendar at the Synod of Whitby in 664. Not that he's necessarily well-remembered for it, or won himself any fans in the process. He is quoted by Bede in his pro-Roman argument at the Synod:

We have learned that Easter is observed by men of different nations and languages at one and the same time, wherever the Church of Christ has spread. The only people who stupidly contend against the whole world are these Scots and their partners in obstinacy the Picts and Britons, who inhabit only a portion of these the two uttermost islands of the ocean.

At that time, Wilfrid was the abbot of a newly founded monastery at Ripon and it's thanks to his European travels that the crypt of this monastery still exists. Buildings in his native Northumbria were made from timber and thatch, but Wilfrid, influenced by the mighty buildings he saw abroad, wanted to build in stone. He decided he would replace the timber building of his monastery with a stone church.

This was no easy matter as the skills of the stonemasons had died out since Roman times. But it's thought that Wilfrid brought some of the craftsmen he needed from Rome and France. And while none of that original church still stands above ground – it was destroyed by fire in the 10th century – the underground crypt is still there. It's down to his determined efforts that a fine example of 7th-century Anglo-Saxon architecture still exists in the UK today.

The story of the crypt and its pilgrims

And what of that crypt – what was it used for and what do we know of the people who visited it from 672 onwards?

They were pilgrims, who came to visit the relics housed here, relics brought by Wilfrid from his travels, long since plundered and gone. They travelled from all over the north of England and approached the building from the west side – and they travelled barefoot. Entering the church, they walked in procession around it and handed over a payment to see the relics before being taken to the steps leading down to the crypt.

At the bottom of the steps they followed the twists and turns of the narrow passageway, winding and weaving and disorientating the walker until it suddenly opened out into a large vaulted chamber. Richly decorated in silk fabrics, jewelled boxes held the relics for

The Crypt. (© *Bernadette Fallon*)

veneration. And a member of the clergy watched closely from the 'monks' window' so that none of the treasures went missing.

The pilgrims kneeled to worship and pray, then made the journey back up the steps on the other side of the crypt, travelling back from the darkness into light. Their journey symbolised the journey from church to the tomb and back to life again, renewed by sacrifice and prayer.

It's still an atmospheric journey in the 21st century, stepping from the bright cathedral nave into the darkened tunnel of steps and the twisting passageways below, emerging into the vaults of an architectural structure that has stood for over thirteen centuries.

But there was more to the crypt than its relics. It also housed a test of chastity for the women of Ripon that can still be seen today – a short flight of steps leading to a small hole in the wall, known as Wilfrid's Needle. Any woman who planned to marry was required to climb the steps and pass through the wall to prove her 'maidenhood'. Any who couldn't fit through were deemed unfit for marriage. The practice lasted until the time of Queen Elizabeth I, who said it was nonsense and put a stop to it.

Why did the cathedral fall down?

Wilfrid's original stone building was destroyed by fire and rebuilding started around 1180. The cathedral that stands today is a mix of styles from several centuries, though parts of it haven't always been standing.

There were problems from the start. The centre tower began to lean even as it was being built and barely thirty years after the west front was finished, the east end fell down. Once this was rebuilt the building was raided by the Scots at the start of the 14th century and set alight. At the start of the 16th century the north and south sides of the nave collapsed. The following century the central spire fell down, causing a lot of damage to the quire.

The church authorities were worried the other spires might fall also, so they decided to remove them. But spires weren't the only things in danger of falling. The foreman on the job was working on the outside of the building, attached by ropes held in place by his workmates. He saw two men racing horses far below on Bondgate Green and, seeing that one of the riders was holding his horse back, cried out 'Let go, let go'. Unfortunately, this confused his colleagues and they let go of the rope. Luckily, he only fell from the spire to the top of the tower and, according to reports, wasn't injured.

As well as various parts of the building falling down, by the mid-19th century huge cracks had started to appear in the west front. The eminent Victorian architect Sir George Gilbert Scott was called in to assess the damage and found things in a bad state. The north-west tower was an empty shell open to the elements and rain was coming through the roof of the nave and transepts. This didn't deter a local builder from storing his timber in the nearby north aisle, and apparently, he also used the space to mix mortar in the winter.

It turned out that the church was built in the wrong place. Not Wilfrid's original church, his considerably smaller building was located on ground that was well capable of supporting it. But as the building grew bigger, it was extended onto sloping sandy ground, not suitable at all for a building of this size and weight. As well as this, the foundations were not deep enough, the rubble-filled walls were weak, the early buttresses were more decorative than functional and competition between stonemasons to create ever more elaborate structures meant the building was being carried out with more enthusiasm than knowledge. Wilfrid's 7th-century builders were using well-tried Roman techniques. Later generations weren't and it showed.

One of Gilbert Scott's first jobs was to create new foundations beneath the original structure, using massive balks of timber to hold everything in place while the masonry was being installed. When the day came to remove the timber supports, the locals gathered to watch the proceedings at a safe distance, convinced the building would come crashing down. But Gilbert Scott's careful stonemasons had done their work well, digging down 14 feet below the original foundations to create the new ones.

Curiouser and curiouser: 'Alice' in the cathedral

One of the most visually stunning parts of the cathedral is the quire and the carvings on the misericord seats here are some of the finest and most interesting you will see anywhere in the country. In fact, they may just have inspired one of the most famous books ever

The quire. (© *Bernadette Fallon*)

written, *Alice in Wonderland* by Lewis Carroll, the pen name of writer Charles Dodgson. Dodgson was very familiar with Ripon and was a frequent visitor to the cathedral as his father, also Charles, was canon there in the 1850s.

One of the carvings shows a griffin chasing a rabbit, which is leaping down a rabbit hole. Did this give him the idea for the story? It's only speculation but seems likely. There is a further link between Ripon and the Alice story. Dodgson negotiated with the Reverend Badcock, principal of Ripon College, for the artist Tenniell to use Badcock's young daughter, Mary, as the model for Alice in his stories.

Don't miss: the animals in the misericords

Many of the misericords feature animals that have taken on human characteristics, with lots of wit and comedy. Many feature obvious religious symbolism – the elephant gripping Judas in his trunk as well as Jonah being cast to the whale and Jonah climbing back to dry land. Others are fantastically playful – a pig playing the bagpipes is maybe a dig at the Scots who had centuries before attacked part of the cathedral, and a friar 'fox' is shown preaching to his rather gullible congregation of a hen and a duck. The Pagan green man makes an appearance and there's a very funny carving of a man pushing his mother in a wheelbarrow.

Curious facts: the 'fake dates' in the quire

It's apparently easy to date the quire stalls in Ripon as 1489 is carved on the misericord seat next to the dean's and 1494 appears in Arabic numerals on the bench end at the bishop's stall. But this is probably one of Gilbert Scott's little jokes, as years later people realised that Arabic numbers weren't in common use back then and, in fact, Ripon didn't have a bishop until 1836 when it received its cathedral status. While the misericords and quire do in fact date from the 1400s, it seems likely that Scott added the dates during his 19th-century restoration.

His restoration work can be easily spotted – watch out for the smoother, darker wood he used. And before you leave the quire, take a look up at the mighty organ and the wooden hand attached to the wall nearby. It can be moved up and down to direct the choir by the organist, a useful tool as the organist's back is turned to them.

Since receiving cathedral status in 1836, the church has added several contemporary 'treasures' to its holdings. Its bronze pulpit dates from 1913 and shows the four famous northern saints, Cuthbert, Chad, Hilda and Etheldreda. St Hilda was the founding abbess of the monastery at Whitby and the three fossils above her head are a reference to the snakes she reportedly banished from the Whitby cliffs. The story proved to have commercial 'legs'. Centuries later enterprising locals carved snakes' heads on ammonite beach fossils and sold them to tourists.

Don't miss: Jesus as a young man

One thing that caused a bit of a stir when it arrived was the high altar reredos, the screen behind the altar. Created in the early 1920s as a memorial for the First World War, the central figure is a very youthful Christ who hasn't even grown a beard yet, a sad reminder of those who died so young. He's flanked by St Michael crushing the serpent and St George killing the dragon. St Wilfrid is on the right and St Peter on the left. The screen is a bit of showmanship, a move away from the austere post-Reformation church furnishings, back to the 'high drama' of the earlier Catholicism.

Step into the Chapel of the Holy Spirit for a wonderful show of contemporary art. The striking metal sculpture by Leslie Durbin captures the energy of Pentecost with its 'tongues of fire' and floating silver pieces, creating in the process a very futuristic design – a cross that could pass for a drone, a planet spinning through time.

Pentecost, the Christian festival celebrating the descent of the Holy Spirit on the disciples of Jesus after his ascension into heaven, meets space exploration.

Don't miss: the Harold Gosney sculptures

The artwork of Harold Gosney, three copper statues of Mary with her son Jesus at various stages of their lives, is a very moving representation of their relationship. Life captured in a snapshot: the new mother cradling her baby, playing with her young son, and heartbrokenly holding his broken body in her arms after his death.

Contemporary art plays a big part in the everyday life of the cathedral. Ripon holds regular exhibitions of local artists and it's

Gosney statue. (© *Bernadette Fallon*)   Art exhibition. (© *Bernadette Fallon*)

not uncommon to find an artist in residence sketching portraits for visitors. It's a way to attract people into the building and provide the funds that are constantly needed for its upkeep.

But to finish we must return to where we began, to Wilfrid. Legend has it that he is buried in the cathedral near the high altar. But is he? We know he died in Northumbria and a letter written after his death claims he is buried in Canterbury. The truth is that nobody knows or now is likely to. But his crypt remains, a lasting testament through so many centuries to his life's work around the world, and the world he brought back here to Ripon.

Visiting Ripon Cathedral

Guides and welcomers are happy to answer your questions and are on duty daily in the cathedral; for more information and opening times visit Riponcathedral.info.

Ripon: where to go and what to do

Ripon is a cathedral city with the welcoming friendliness of a market town and it is those two aspects of its character for which it is best known. Because you can't miss the cathedral, rising out of the wide sweep of the road near the river, it's a commanding presence in a compact city, one of Britain's smallest.

And its market square tradition still functions in the same way it has done for centuries. Every night at 9 pm the horn-blower sounds his horn at each corner of the obelisk in the square to set the night watch. It's a ritual that dates back over a thousand years and evolved from the role of the wakeman of the city. The original wakeman, a type of mayor, was appointed to make sure the residents were safely home by curfew, particularly important in Medieval times when northern towns were under threat of marauding raids from the Scots.

Ripon shared in Yorkshire's prosperity in the wool trade in the 12th century and its cloth industry was one of the biggest in the county. This was partly due to the proximity of Fountains Abbey, a Cistercian monastery just outside the town, and the Cistercians' long tradition of sheep farming. The abbey also owned a lot of grazing land, suitable for sheep and the production of wool, but was sacked during the Reformation and its abbot expelled.

Today's Fountains Abbey is one of the largest and best preserved Cistercian ruins in the country and a World Heritage Site, providing an insight into spiritual life in Medieval times. In the grounds you'll also see the stunning Studley Royal Water Garden, created in the 18th century in the 'English' garden style. Here you'll find elegant ponds and cascades with rustic bridges and classical temples and statues. It's a pleasant walk from Ripon for the energetic, at just over 3 miles, some of which winds scenically along the river.

Also in the area is Newby Hall, one of Britain's finest 'Adam' houses, built originally in the 1690s by Sir Christopher Wren, later enlarged and adapted by Robert Adam to create a stunning 18th-century interior. Particularly worth a look are the Statue Gallery, Library and Tapestry Room – and of course the gardens, with the miniature railway and adventure playground for children.

You can take a cruise to the hall on Ripon Canal, which dates from 1769 and was a busy trade route for the city for almost 100 years until the railway opened. It was renovated and re-opened by local organisations in 1996 and extended right into the centre of Ripon. Tours now operate on the canal and boats are also available for private hire.

Ripley Castle, despite the name, is a Grade 1 listed 14th-century country house between Ripley and Harrogate. Privately owned, it has been the seat of the Ingleby baronets for centuries and is open to the public for guided tours.

You'll find the Ripon Spa Gardens in the heart of the city, close to the cathedral, with its eye-catching tree sculptures of some of the characters from Lewis Carroll's *Alice in Wonderland*. There's a very pleasant café here, a Victorian bandstand that hosts concerts in the summer months and a Green Man Trail, with thirty green man plaques hidden among the trees and flowerbeds in the gardens.

If you're visiting the cathedral there's no question where you should stay – it has to be the Old Deanery just opposite. With front-facing bedrooms overlooking the imposing church architecture, the building dates back to 1625 and is the former home of the deans of Ripon. It's packed full of period details, such as the impressive original oak staircase, and individual quirks like the gently sloping floorboards. There are just eleven rooms in total, each one completely individual, and the hotel is full of character and cosiness. You too can experience the life of a dean for a day.

Ripon's nearest large centre is Harrogate, an easy drive or bus journey, with a good local bus service running regularly throughout the day. From Harrogate, it's easy to get to Leeds, Bradford or York, where you'll find national connections by train or bus to the rest of the country. Historically part of the West Riding of Yorkshire, Ripon is a great base from which to explore the Yorkshire Dales.

Chapter 4

Wakefield

From doorstep to mighty monument: the history of Wakefield Cathedral

Wakefield Cathedral. (© *Wakefield Cathedral: reproduced by kind permission*)

The spire of Wakefield Cathedral is the tallest in Yorkshire. At 75 metres, it dominates the skyline for miles around. But the honour of marking the area as a place of Christian worship for 1,000 years goes to a much smaller and more humble monument. So humble, in fact, it was discovered being used as a lowly doorstep in a barber's shop in Westgate back in the 1800s.

The Saxon cross shaft dates to the middle of the 10th century, and though its original location is not known, it's likely it stood somewhere close to the cathedral. It was a central symbol of Christian faith in Anglo-Saxon times and would have been a focus for worship and gathering before the church was built.

Today the original, rescued from its life in a doorway, is in the care of the Wakefield Museum, though you will find a contemporary Saxon cross based on this original design outside the cathedral. It has been carved, as it would have been back then, by hand with a hammer and chisel.

The bodies in the cathedral

Aside from the cross, the beginnings of this holy site can be dated to at least 1000, due to the discovery of two important cist burials in the south aisle of the cathedral nave in 2012, during the cathedral's current redevelopment programme. The earliest burial in this Medieval stone-lined grave has been radiocarbon-dated to between 970 and 1150. The people buried here would almost certainly have worshipped at the original Saxon cross outside.

Redevelopment and renewal have been a constant in the building's history. A church at Wakefield was recorded in the *Domesday Book* in 1086 and, while the current building didn't receive cathedral status until 1888, the story of its creation starts around 1088.

You will see its entire 900-year history spread out before you when you step through the west entrance, under the mighty spire. Light pouring in, a new Yorkshire sandstone floor, cleaned and repointed walls, the stunning labyrinth – these are all modern creations. But ironically these 'new' improvements have restored the church to the glory days of its Medieval past when it functioned as a flexible space, a meeting place and venue for the local community, just like it is today.

The story of the labyrinth

The intriguing labyrinth spread out at your feet at the entrance is new to the building but the concept of the labyrinth isn't. It predates

Labyrinth. (© *Wakefield Cathedral: reproduced by kind permission*)

Christianity and has its roots in Pagan cultures. References to labyrinths can be traced back to early Crete, Egypt, Peru and India and labyrinth designs have been found all over the world, from the walls of caves to ancient pottery fragments. They are sometimes known as sacred gateways and have been found at the entrance to ancient sites around the world.

They have always been associated with ancient pilgrimage routes and rituals of self-discovery, so it's not surprising they became a central feature in many European Roman Catholic churches in the Middle Ages. The most famous of these is in Chartres Cathedral in France, and dates from around 1200. It's fitting that Wakefield has recaptured a historic Christian symbol for contemporary use in this ancient building that is now a modern cathedral.

While sometimes portrayed as mazes or confusing spaces, labyrinths are more commonly 'unicursal', meaning they only have one path leading to the centre and one path out. So unlike a maze, which is designed to trick you, labyrinths are designed to guide you.

Described as a 'path of prayer', walking the labyrinth is a way to still the mind, ground the body, quicken the spirit, open the heart and inspire creativity. It's designed to remind us of the important things in life. We follow the path to the centre and take the same path back, transformed, to our daily lives.

Medieval pilgrims followed the path of the labyrinth on their knees as a means of prayer, symbolising the journey of the soul through life. Today, you probably won't find anyone travelling the path 'by knee', but visitors are welcome to take off their shoes if they like. And unlike the pilgrims of old, they will enjoy the luxury of the cathedral's underfloor heating to ease their journey through it.

Curious facts: the 'twist' in the nave

Look down along the length of the cathedral and you will notice that the line of the building beyond the chancel arch bends slightly to the right. Most Norman churches built in the shape of a cross have this peculiarity and it's something to look out for. The twist represents the head of the dead Christ hanging sideways on the cross and reveals the origin of this cathedral. It tells us it grew out a simple but highly typical 11th-century Norman church, shaped like a cross with a central tower. However, the central tower fell down at the turn of the 14th century, taking part of the building with it.

The north section of the nave with its six arches is the oldest part of the building and dates from 1150. That building was much lower than the one that stands today, as you will see from the marks in the wall. Originally, the arches here were rounded, but were replaced by pointed arches after the central tower collapsed in 1320.

The nave's southern arcade, with its seven pointed arches, was built about 1230. The pillars here are alternately round and octagonal, an architectural feature typical of the reign of Henry III. These pillars are now twice their original height, as you can see if you look closely

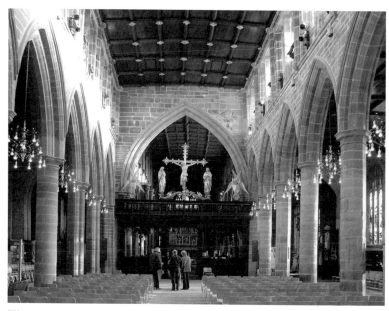

The nave. (© *Wakefield Cathedral: reproduced by kind permission*)

at the stones. The bottom half is made up of semi-circular blocks, the top of whole blocks.

The growth of the building maps the growth of Wakefield as it became a prosperous market town. Its position at the river crossing made it a key player in the developing wool trade and the River Calder became an important route for exporting Yorkshire wool and cloth to the continent. Thriving merchants needed a fine church to show off their town's importance and the growing town needed more space to worship.

But over-rapid development and badly planned extensions caused the tower to fall down. This created another period of rebuilding and growth, and the new tower and spire were added between 1409 and 1420. And while the spire was rebuilt in the 1860s, the main structure of the tower remains as it was built 550 years ago.

The period of the Wars of the Roses from 1455 to 1485, which included the Battle of Wakefield and saw ferocious fighting in the area, constituted the most ambitious development of the church in its history. The entire eastern half of the original Medieval church dates from this time.

Inside the church there were at least five altars by 1483 where priests offered prayers for the wealthy patrons who had endowed these chantry chapels. The clerestory windows above the arches were added as the building expanded to let in more light. By the end of the century the church had grown to such a size that there were twenty-five priests attached to it.

By the end of the 17th century, the church was so crowded that a triple-decker pulpit had to be installed so that the preacher could see out over all the family pews and galleries that had been built for the ever-swelling population. Today's pulpit is the top portion of that 17th-century creation. Lawsuits were taken as families jostled for space to worship. Windows were blocked with the galleries. The pressure weakened the building and, in 1714, the top of the spire blew down in a storm. It remained 20 foot shorter for the next 150 years.

By the mid-1800s, records show that the church had to accommodate seating for up to 1,700 adults, 600 children and host an entire parish population of over 9,000. It was time to address the structural problems and architect George Gilbert Scott was employed to restore and redesign the building. The spire was rebuilt, the galleries were removed and by the time the restoration was complete in 1874, the church's interior was very much as we see it today.

The gilded bosses on the roof of the nave are mostly Medieval, though the panels are Victorian. In a nicely balancing twist, the roofs in the aisle are Medieval with Victorian bosses. They date from the rule of Richard III in the 15th century and trace his history from his time as the Duke of York. You'll also see other royal symbols here including the lion of England and the rose of York, as well as the earliest known example of the arms of the town of Wakefield.

Don't miss: the rood screen

One of the best examples of the evolving styles of the ages can be found in the rood screen, dividing the nave of the cathedral from the quire and sanctuary. It's a remarkable mix of dates and styles but it comes together in a very eye-catching whole. The panels at the bottom are from the Medieval period, given a Victorian restoration, and date from the 1490s. The middle section is made from dark oak and was constructed in 1635. There would have been gates in the original construction and, luckily, these still exist, they're just not here any more. Now they sit in the south quire at the entrance to the Lady Chapel.

Rood screen. (© *Wakefield Cathedral: reproduced by kind permission*)

Because of the destruction of statues and iconography during the Reformation, the Medieval statues that would have stood at the top of the rood are long gone. Today's elaborate gallery and figures on top of the screen were created by J. Ninian Comper, who lived from 1860 to 1964, and show Christ on the cross with the Blessed Virgin and St John the Evangelist.

Owl in quire. (© *Bernadette Fallon*)

Medieval rood screens had a walkway below the figures, accessed by a stairway. To the left of the figures you can still see the original doorway into the Medieval loft, which was removed along with the figures in the Reformation. And if you look very closely you'll see the remains of a Medieval angel painted on a side wall here.

The quire with its beautiful stalls, misericords and carvings was created on the wishes of a bridegroom, Sir Thomas Savil, to celebrate his marriage to Margaret Bosworth in 1482 – and he supplied the money along with the desire. Their respective coats of arms are carved at the end of the stall by the bishop's throne, as well as the rather beautiful carving of an owl, his family symbol, on one of the bench ends.

Don't miss: the 'flasher' in the quire

Just like the rood screen, the misericords in the quire offer a variety of styles. Twenty-five are the originals from the 15th century and fourteen date from the 19th century. Here you'll find the usual mix of stories being told, from the sacred to the profane. The 'mooning man' is a regular favourite with children – a bare-bottomed juggler peeping out through his legs – though a later craftsman added a fig leaf to a 'central' part of the carving to modify the impact of his nakedness. Here too you'll find the Pagan green man.

The modern part of the church starts in the sanctuary and dates from 1905. The flat nave roof gives way to the vaulted ceiling and the majestic effect is continued by the high altar, an elaborate affair in oak, depicting seven orders of angels. Behind it the reredos, created in 1896, was moved to this position in 1905 and again shows off a variety of old and new work. The crucifixion panels are Italian in style, while below, the panels depicting the Last Supper and the Supper at Emmaus, are thought to date from the 16th century. The left-hand panel, showing the Passover, brings us back to modernity and the start of the 20th century.

Don't miss: the Madonna and Child

There is a beautiful contemporary representation of the Madonna and Child in the Lady Chapel, carved from Cadeby limestone by Ian Judd in 1986. It stands alongside the rather bedraggled effigy of William de Melton that dates from Victorian times and was previously outside on a gable. In 1329, William, as Archbishop of York, was

Madonna and child. (© *Bernadette Fallon*)

the man responsible for reconsecrating the building following its extensive redevelopment work after the central tower fell down. Ten years earlier he had faced Robert the Bruce on the battlefield at Myton-on-Swale, leading the army that fought the Scots. Back then bishops were often close companions to the king, and men of action as well as men of prayer.

Curious facts: raising money for a bishop

St Mark's Chapel could be said to be the 'heart' of the cathedral, as it was created following the building's elevation to cathedral status in 1888, as a memorial to the first Bishop of Wakefield, William Walsham How. Interestingly, the cathedral received its status in 1878, but it was ten years before the diocese could raise enough money to enthrone its first bishop.

Several depictions of the famous northern saints are found in this chapel. Their glass panels were originally intended to be attached to the side of the reredos, but they didn't fit when it was relocated in 1905, so they were moved here. Here are the saints Oswald (holding a raven), Chad (holding a model of Lichfield Cathedral), Cuthbert (carrying Oswald's head), John of Beverley, Alcuin and Wilfrid.

You'll also encounter a 'mouse' at the right-hand end of the altar rail, just around the height of your knees on the kneeler. He's the work of Robert Thompson of Kilburn who created most of the furniture in this chapel. There are fifteen other carved mice in the cathedral for you to find.

On the wall of the tower buttress is an old chain leaded into the wall that formerly had an iron collar attached to it. The collar was known as a 'joug' and had a hinge, which allowed it to be closed round the necks of those who are described in cathedral literature as 'scolds' or 'gossips'. Wakefield's stocks were situated just outside the churchyard.

Wakefield's first bishop, William Walsham How, died in 1897 and his marble effigy lies in the Walsham How Chapel in the south aisle, where you'll also find a plaque naming all of the bishops of Wakefield. In this chapel you'll also find a replica that brings you full circle, right back to the origins of this contemporary cathedral – the original Saxon cross that first marked this spot as a holy site over 1,000 years ago.

Visiting the cathedral

Visits to the cathedral are self-guided though informal tours are available on a weekly basis. For more information and opening times visit Wakefieldcathedral.org.

Wakefield: where to go and what to do

Wakefield Cathedral is a great place to start your visit to the city. Not only is it one of most famous and awe-inspiring attractions in the area, it also houses the friendly visitor centre, which is run by very knowledge staff.

This West Yorkshire city is located on the edge of the Pennines on the River Calder, an important trading position that brought it great wealth in the 19th century. Fortunes declined in the later part of the 20th century, as manufacturing and mining industries stopped production and the Wakefield coal mines were among the first in the country to close in the 1980s.

Fortunately, like so many other parts of northern England, Wakefield has kick-started its regeneration in the 21st century, with new investment and building developments. Parts of its former glory have been transformed for modern living. Both the Wakefield Westgate Station yard and the waterfront area along the river and canal have been converted into places to shop, work and live.

One of the most important cultural developments in this area has been the opening of The Hepworth Wakefield, an art gallery named in honour of local sculptor Barbara Hepworth, exhibiting much of her work. Barbara Hepworth was born in Wakefield in 1903. Another famous local sculptor, Henry Moore, is also featured in the gallery, alongside other prominent British and international artists.

It hasn't all been redeveloped, of course. Take a historical walk around the city to admire the Grade II listed Neoclassical Crown Court of 1810, Wakefield Town Hall, which dates from 1880, and the Country Hall of 1898, built in the Queen Anne style.

You can trace the history of the area in an impressive contemporary building, the £31 million Wakefield One, which houses Wakefield Museum and the library. Among its treasures is a collection of preserved animals, brought to the UK by Victorian explorer Charles Waterton that includes a South American crocodile. He created what was the world's first nature reserve at his home in Walton Hall, a Palladian-style stately home on the outskirts of Wakefield. It was built on the site of a former Medieval hall with its own moat. Today it's a hotel called Waterton Park, the ideal place to stay when visiting the cathedral.

For a look back into the area's mining history – including a chance to descend 140 metres under the ground into one of the oldest coal mines in Britain – the National Coal Mining Museum for England is within driving distance of Wakefield. Tours reveal what the working life of the mines was like for the men, women and – yes – children who worked in them.

Or travel even further back in time, to the Wars of the Roses and Sandal Castle to the south of the city centre. Here, in the Battle of Wakefield in 1460, Richard, Duke of York, was killed. In fact, in the famous nursery rhyme it's thought to be to Sandal Castle that he was marching up to:

Oh, the grand old Duke of York, he had ten thousand men
He marched them up to the top of the hill and he marched them
down again

Today only the castle's ruins, motte and bailey are all that's left but you can still climb the steps to the top of the motte for stunning views over the valley and the Calder river.

Another link with the great wars that changed the course of English history can be found at the nearby ruined Pontefract Castle, which was used as a Lancastrian stronghold and a base for the troops marching into the Battle of Wakefield. But it's even more famous for being the place where Richard II was imprisoned and died in 1400. Today it's still not known if he starved himself to death with grief at being deposed as king by Henry Bolingbroke, who became King Henry IV, or was left to starve by his captors. Other famous prisoners include James I of Scotland, and Charles d'Orleans, captured at the Battle of Agincourt in 1415. In general it's had a bloody history. It was also used by the Duke of Gloucester, who became Richard III in 1483, as one of his official residences. In fact, he had several of his political opponents executed there.

But the city that played such an important role in Britain's history also has a quirky link with nature. Wakefield is the capital of the rhubarb triangle, an area famous for producing early rhubarb. A festival in spring celebrates its connection, the Wakefield Festival of Food, Drink and Rhubarb.

The city has very good rail and road links to nearby Leeds, Bradford and Sheffield, and Leeds-Bradford International Airport is just under a 20-mile drive.

Chapter 5

Sheffield

Power, intrigue and politics in Sheffield Cathedral

Sheffield Cathedral. (© *Sheffield Cathedral: reproduced by kind permission*)

Political intrigue and power struggles. Royal prisoners. England's most famous cardinal on the run. A queen in bondage. Sheffield has seen it all and the cathedral has been central to much of the action.

But consider this. If you view cathedrals as remote lofty spaces, standing apart from modern times and outside contemporary culture, a visit to Sheffield may cure you. As the Dean of Sheffield puts it, a cathedral is a public space and can only exist if there are partnerships and friendships, because any effort to build a community cannot be done alone.

A 'public community space' it certainly is. The lightweight seating has even been chosen for its mobility so it can be stacked to one side when the cathedral is opened up for functions and concerts, as it so often is. And within these walls that contain stones dating back to Norman times, you will find the history of the changing community of Sheffield over 1,000 years.

The making of a cathedral

Back then it wasn't a cathedral. It didn't become one until 1914 in fact, making it a double celebration when it re-opened its doors in 2014 after extensive renovations, a modern rebirth and a centenary birthday. It's the oldest building still in use in Sheffield and it's come a long way from the site that was first marked for spiritual purposes by a Saxon cross – the 'Sheffield Cross' – 1,000 years ago. The cathedral tells the story of Sheffield, from its origins in the early 12th century when William de Lovetot built the first church on this site.

Today you'll have to go to the British Museum in London to see the Sheffield Cross. But don't worry. There's still plenty to see in the cathedral, from ancient monuments to modern art, right from the minute you step through the doors.

And stepping through the doors is a bit of a shock to the senses, as 1960s modernity and 21st-century art lead to a Victorian nave with the signs of centuries of rebuilding etched out in the east wall. The ultra-modern glass entrance porch leads to a bright, open space that was rebuilt in the 1960s to allow more light into the building. The contemporary stainless steel baptismal font is by artist and metalworker Brian Fell, while the ceilings beyond date from the 19th century.

The main part of the nave dates from Victorian times, but you can still see the earlier rooflines in the east wall. The nave leads to the

The nave. (© *Sheffield Cathedral: reproduced by kind permission*)

Medieval part of the building, the chancel, sanctuary, tower and spire, built in the early 15th century. Here the ceilings date from the 1400s, as do the soaring gilded angels above. Though not the angels' wings. They were added in the 1960s, a gift from the cathedral architect.

Curious facts: the cathedra

In this part of the building you'll find the bishop's throne, the 'cathedra', from where the word cathedral comes. According to local history, the cathedra was gifted by one of the candidates for the newly created post of bishop after the church was granted cathedral status in 1914. He didn't get the job.

It's a beautiful oak seat though, gilded and carved with the figures of Saint Peter, Saint Paul and Christ, celebrating the building's official name – the Cathedral Church of St Peter and St Paul. There's a pelican at the top, which is a Christian symbol of sacrifice, and we're even treated to a view of sacrifice in action as the bird pecks its breast to feed its young with drops of its own blood.

The chancel. (© *Sheffield Cathedral: reproduced by kind permission*)

You'll also find the canons' stalls here at the back of the chancel, with their beautifully carved wooden Victorian misericords. What you won't find, unlike other cathedrals, is the choir. Traditionally cathedral choirs sing from the ornate Medieval stalls, also known as the quire. But in Sheffield they sing from the modern nave, seated on the light contemporary pews of the 21st century, in an effort to bring the heart of the church into the heart of the congregation, another manifestation of community integration at work in this modern-day cathedral.

History in the sanctuary

The sanctuary is the most easterly part of the original church and the most sacred part of the cathedral. This is the oldest part of the building, dating back to around 1430. It was originally built in the shape of a cross, with a tower and spire rising above, a feature that has dominated Sheffield for 600 years.

Look up at the east wall and you'll see some of the oldest stones in the church. You'll be able to spot them easily because of their zig-zag design. These stones date back to the early 12th century and came from the original Norman church on the site. It's thought that this church was destroyed along with Sheffield Castle during the 13th century.

The sanctuary's east window, behind the high altar, is a memorial to James Montgomery, who lived from 1771 to 1854, was a newspaper editor, social reformer, anti-slavery campaigner, supporter of the Sunday School movement AND wrote the famous Christmas hymn *Angels from the Realms of Glory*. The window shows St Matthew, Moses, David and St John, and was given to the cathedral by the Mappin family. Famous local manufacturers of Sheffield silverware and cutlery, their very distinguished client list included Marie Antoinette, the last Czar of Russia Nicholas II, Charles Dickens and Winston Churchill.

There are memorials to three former Sheffield vicars, Rev Thomas Sale, Rev James Wilkinson and Rev Thomas Sutton, on the wall of the sanctuary, though it's not clear how happy Wilkinson and Montgomery would be to share this space. Rev Wilkinson, who was also a Justice of the Peace, had James Montgomery imprisoned for sedition when Montgomery criticised him for forcibly dispersing a political protest in the town. During his time as vicar he also turned John Wesley away from speaking at the church pulpit in 1779, driving him out into nearby Paradise Square to the north of the cathedral, where a large crowd gathered to hear him.

Curious facts: the earls, the cardinal and the queen

One of the most interesting parts of the cathedral, full of stories of political wrangling, betrayal and despair, is the Shrewsbury Chapel, which was added to the building around 1520 by the Lord of the Manor of Sheffield, George Talbot, 4th Earl of Shrewsbury. His ancestor, John Talbot, the 1st Lord of Shrewsbury, was a famous soldier and the Talbot of Shakespeare's *Henry VI Part 1*.

It was built to be a private family chapel with a burial vault underneath, a vault with a curious mystery. But more of that later. The earl's effigy lies on a marble and alabaster platform, flanked on either side by a wife – his first wife Anne, who was married to him for twenty years, and his second wife Elizabeth, who outlived him and in fact paid for the tomb. The earl is dressed in the robes of a Knight of the Garter, and his two countesses wear their coronets and robes.

The earl, who lived until 1538, was the first of the Shrewsbury family to make his home in the city, living in Sheffield Castle and building Manor Lodge in nearby Deer Park. He hosted Cardinal Wolsey in the lodge for two weeks, when the cardinal was making his way back to London in disgrace after being arrested for high treason in York. Wolsey had fallen out of favour with Henry VIII after failing to persuade the pope to grant the divorce from Catherine of Aragon that would leave Henry free to marry Anne Boleyn.

George Shrewsbury and wives. (© *Sheffield Cathedral: reproduced by kind permission*)

Sheffield may well have been the cardinal's undoing, as, while he was lodged with the Earl of Shrewsbury, the Constable of the Tower of London arrived with twenty-four Tower guards, a likely sign that he was to be executed. Wolsey had been ill with suspected cholera but now became even weaker.

Technically he wasn't a guest in the lodge but a prisoner, even though the earl, in his compassion and hospitality, refused to acknowledge it. Wolsey's biographer and friend George Cavendish accompanied him to Sheffield and writes of the Cardinal's sympathetic reception in the city:

And the next day we removed and rode to Sheffield Park, where my Lord of Shrewsbury lay within the lodge, the people all the way thitherward still lamenting him, crying as they did before. And when we came into the park, nigh to the lodge, my Lord of Shrewsbury with my lady and a train of gentlewomen, and all other his gentlemen and servants, stood without the gates to attend my Lord's coming, to receive him.

At whose alighting the Earl received him with much honour, and embraced my lord, saying these words: 'My Lord, your Grace is most heartily welcome unto me, and I am glad to see you here in my poor lodge, where I have long desired to see you, and should have been much more gladder if you had come after another sort.'

'Ay, my gentle Lord of Shrewsbury,' said my Lord, 'I heartily thank you and although I have cause to lament, yet as a faithful heart may, I do rejoice that my chance is to come unto the custody of so noble a person. I beseech God to help me'.

'My Lord,' replied Shrewsbury, 'be of good cheer and fear not, for I will not receive you as a prisoner but as my good Lord, and the King's true and faithful subject.'

Wolsey wasn't long for this world. After eighteen days in Sheffield he continued his sad journey southwards to Nottingham and then to Leicester Abbey, where he died.

The 4th Earl was not the only member of the Shrewsbury family asked to host a royal prisoner. On the other side of the chapel is the equally magnificent tomb of George, 6th Earl of Shrewsbury, who was given the job of custodian to Mary Queen of Scots by her cousin Queen Elizabeth I. Elizabeth wanted her out of Scotland where Mary was said to be plotting against her. Her stay in Sheffield was considerably longer though. She lived between Manor Lodge and the castle for fourteen years.

History and intrigue aside, there's a moving human story behind it all. It was said that looking after Queen Mary nearly ruined the earl financially. And, despite the fact he was married to Elizabeth, better known as Bess of Hardwych, who was the richest woman in England after the queen, it is said that he fell in love with Mary. Which makes you feel for his suffering as he was forced to watch her eventual execution.

Bess was his second wife, he was her fourth husband. But the family line didn't continue much further. His son, the 7th Earl of Shrewsbury, died leaving no sons so the Sheffield estates were

4th Earl of Shrewsbury. (© *Sheffield Cathedral: reproduced by kind permission*)

inherited by his daughter, Alethea Talbot. She was married to Thomas Howard, from the family who rose so high in the reign of King Henry VIII to become the Earls of Arundel, Surrey and Norfolk. The Sheffield lands were absorbed into the House of Howard and the Talbot line with it.

Curious facts: the missing bodies

But the earl's title is not all that's missing from Sheffield these days. There was a bit of a local sensation several years ago when the family crypt was opened and it was discovered that fifteen bodies were missing, including the three earls. Where did they go?

According to historical records, it was discovered that not all of the lead coffins buried in the family crypt were present when it was opened once before in the 19th century. It's thought they were taken to provide lead shot for muskets during the 17th-century civil war, or maybe even for repairs of the lead roof.

So while you won't find the earls of Shrewsbury in the crypt, you will find a reference to them at the coronation of the British monarch. When Henry VIII dissolved the monasteries and took over their lands, he allowed the chapel of nearby Worksop on the earl's lands to be retained for the people of the parish. In return, the earl promised that his family would always gift a white glove at the monarch's coronation. In the coronation of Queen Elizabeth II in 1953, you will see she is wearing a white glove as she holds the sceptre. So the tradition remains.

Curious facts: a Catholic chapel in an Anglican cathedral

The Shrewsbury Chapel remained true to its Roman Catholic origins for several hundred years after the Reformation and continued as a private Catholic chapel within this Anglican cathedral until 1933.

Then it was given by the Duke of Norfolk, into whose hands it had passed, to the cathedral for the use of the parishioners.

Just in front of the Shrewsbury Chapel is the Lady Chapel, decorated with carved bosses that date from the Medieval period. Here you'll find the popular green man and another very striking Pagan image, the Sheela-na-gig. This is described in the cathedral guidebook as 'an exaggerated female form', which is a politer way than she is usually described, as a naked woman displaying a very large vulva.

A mass clock on the south wall of the Lady Chapel dates from the 13th century and is a type of sundial that would originally have been on an outside wall of the building. This told the people of Sheffield when it was time to come to church. This part of the church was rebuilt in the 15th century when, apparently, the clock was moved inside.

Curious facts: some unfinished business

The area of the chancel, sanctuary, tower and spire is part of the original layout of the Medieval parish church, built in the Perpendicular style like so many other English churches. But that's not the only layout you'll find in this building, though the more recent one is only half-finished and adds its own personality to the mix of architectural stories that Sheffield cathedral tells.

After the then parish church of Sheffield was designated a cathedral in 1914, it was felt the building wasn't grand enough for its new classification and so work began to extend it. The layout, as is traditional in most UK churches, runs from west to east and further extension was blocked in both directions by existing buildings outside. Instead it was decided to 'turn' the focus instead and extend the building from north to south.

Work started and part of the new nave was created on the north side of the cathedral, but the First World War prevented it going any further and the extension was never completed. Which means today the cathedral has the rather odd shape an unfinished nave provides – extending to the north but not to the south.

Don't miss: St George's Chapel

On the plus side this has created plenty of space for St George's Chapel and the new military chapel of St Michael and St George. Created as a memorial for the York and Lancaster Regiment, it also commemorates the city's links with HMS *Sheffield*. HMS *Sheffield* is very much a product of the city it comes from with its strong steel heritage. It's even known as the 'Shiny Sheff' because of the amount of stainless steel used in its construction, instead of the traditional brass.

The dignified memorials in this part of the cathedral bring a lump to the throat with their reminders of sacrifice, bloodshed and death. The 12th (Sheffield City) Battalion of the York and Lancaster Regiment lost many of its members on 1 July 1916, only two years

St George's Chapel. (© *Sheffield Cathedral: reproduced by kind permission*)

after its formation, on the first day of the Battle of the Somme. The wooden seats are carved in memory of some of those who lost their lives and three cases under the stained-glass windows hold the regiment's Rolls of Honour from 1914 to 1968.

The old St George's Chapel holds the stained-glass window of the Six Sheffield Worthies, soldiers who were associated with the city's history from the 11th to the 17th centuries. The ceiling here is decorated with the white and red roses of York and Lancaster. While you're in this chapel, take time to admire the cross high up on the north wall, placed there, as your guide will be proud to tell you, by the 80-year-old Bishop Burrows who climbed up a 75-foot ladder with it.

Don't miss: the windows in the south aisle

The four memorial windows in the south aisle have an interesting history. They were removed and stored in Nunnery Colliery for the duration of the Second World War, to keep them safe from the bombing. Sheffield, with its steelworks, was a key military target. Unfortunately, the pumps installed to pump away the water that naturally seeps into deep collieries failed and the colliery was flooded with acidic water, dissolving both the wooden cases storing the windows and the leadwork holding them together. When the windows were recovered, all that was left was a pile of several hundred pieces of glass and it took twelve years to re-assemble it all in the correct order. Fortunately, the restorer had kept photos and drawings of the four windows and was able to reconstruct the correct patterns and restore them intact to the community.

Because, despite all of the noble, royal and military histories represented around the cathedral, it is community that today's cathedral is most noted for. A living, breathing part of Sheffield, entwined in its past, with a firm foothold in its future. With many fascinating stories to tell along the way.

Visiting the cathedral

One-hour guided tours are available and can be pre-booked. For more information and opening times visit Sheffieldcathedral.org.

Sheffield: where to go and what to do

It's difficult to spend any time in Sheffield without being aware of the city's steel heritage. If West Yorkshire trade is built on wool, the south is built on steel and iron. From the 18th to the 20th centuries, the region was the industrial centre of northern England, blessed with the riches of iron ore, coal and water that caused its industry to flourish.

But what happens to a city when its industry dies? Often it dies too, but not so in Sheffield, a thriving heart of the north. So even though the pits and steelworks of Barnsley and Doncaster have closed, some have been regenerated for new uses, like the museums and exhibition centres that tell the story of their former glory. The city's great buildings, created by the wealth of Victorian patronage, remain. And their number is growing. Today the steel you'll see in Sheffield is on the cranes and scaffoldings of buildings as the city goes through a period of urban renewal and revitalisation.

There are plenty of places to trace the history of steel around the city, including the Metalwork Gallery, charting today's transformation of the industry. The gallery is part of the larger Millennium Gallery, comprising spaces that include the Ruskin Gallery collections of paintings, drawings and manuscripts established and inspired by the eminent Victorian critic, artist, writer and philosopher John Ruskin.

The Winter Gardens in the city centre is a stunning public space with an innovative glass roof supported by laminated arches. It contrasts nicely with the Victorian façade of the nearby town hall, where old and new Sheffield sit beautifully together. On a sunny day the Peace Gardens with its fountains, lawns and sculptures make a visually inspiring backdrop for a picnic.

Travel out to the Abbeydale Industrial Hamlet, a few miles south-west of the city, for a look back at the history of steelworks when it was just a cottage industry. Here you can explore restored 18th century forges, workshops and machines.

Also located a few miles out of the city, Meersbrook Park offers a pretty view over Sheffield and a lot of mature woodland and walks. It was originally the grounds to Meersbrook Hall and now you'll find the Bishops' House here. It's a fine example of a 15th-century timber-framed house, run as a local museum, with connections to the Blythe bishops of Sheffield. However, nobody can confirm that the bishops actually lived here.

You'll find less tourists in Sheffield than you will in many other cathedral cities in the country, but you will find lots of students and friendly locals who give the city its lively, welcoming atmosphere. It's a well-connected city with regular rail links to the north of England and London.

Chapter 6

Bradford

Yorkshire's hidden gem: Bradford Cathedral

It was hardly an illustrious recording. Bradford, the *Domesday Book*, 1086:

Ilbert hath it. It is waste.

But from those inauspicious beginnings, Bradford has grown from a crossing place that became a market to an important industrial town and multi-cultural city. And the city's cathedral, which received its status in 1919, reflects this history throughout the building with its memorials, shrines and stories.

There is no mention of a church in the *Domesday Book* but it is likely that the Ilbert de Lacy mentioned, the Norman lord of the area, would have had a chapel on his manor. The earliest findings on today's cathedral site are two carved stones, thought to be part of a Saxon preaching cross that suggest this place was used for Christian worship as far back as the 7th century.

A wooden church from this time was destroyed in the 11th century, following the Norman invasion, and replaced with a stone church in the year 1200. There is an entry in the register of the Archbishop of York in 1281 recording a grant from Alice de Lacy, widow of one of Ilbert's descendants, to the parish of Bradford and by 1283 a vicar is named.

Bradford Cathedral. (© *Bernadette Fallon*)

The wooden church didn't last, however, plundered and burned by Scottish raiders at the start of the following century. Fire-blackened stones and the foundations of earlier buildings were found during the building's extension work in the 1960s. The findings suggest that the first stone church was about half the size of the present nave.

The nave today dates from 1458 and is the oldest part of the building. It's accessed from the West End entrance, through the tower that was built in 1508. The clock didn't come until nearly a century later and was installed in 1666, the first public clock in Bradford.

The nave. (© *Bernadette Fallon*)

The tower stands over 100 feet high and has twelve bells, ten of which were re-cast in memory of the local men who fought in the two world wars. It's not the only memory of war the tower carries. During the Civil War sieges in the early 1640s when Royalist forces attacked the town, the tower became a stronghold against cannon-fire and woolsacks were hung outside to protect it. Cannonballs have since been dug up at the foot of the tower.

The ancient marks in the tower

We can trace the tower's history back even further. Alongside the spiral staircase that rises to the bells, you'll see a stone that bears the date 1281, marked by the mason who worked on it. Other masons' marks are also clear on the massive old walls of the tower.

Congregations began to swell in the 18th century as the town's prosperity grew. Temporary galleries to provide extra seating were added on all four sides of the nave, as well as a false ceiling. You can still see the marks where they were installed above the windows. Here too you'll see brightly coloured angels, supporting the beams of the roof. A very eye-catching feature, they're linked with Kirkstall Abbey, a ruined Cistercian monastery north-west of Leeds, founded in 1152 and disestablished during Henry VIII's Dissolution of the Monasteries.

Overseen by bishops, run by clergy, governed by local dignitaries, the history of the church in centuries past is one usually ruled by men. So it's interesting to see a colourful celebration of 'girl power' at the entrance to Bradford cathedral. The 'Women of the Bible' window was installed in 1863 by a Bradford solicitor in memory of his sisters. The Catherine and Jane Wells Memorial Window shows famous scenes of women in Christianity, including the Angel Gabriel greeting Mary, Mary Magdalene with the risen Christ, Jesus with the sisters Mary and Martha of Bethany, and Jesus speaking with the woman at the well.

There's another striking feature to look out for here – the font. Typically installed at the entrance to a church to symbolise entry into the Christian faith through baptism, the Bradford font has a very unusual feature. The intricately designed wooden canopy was

Bradford angels. (© *Bernadette Fallon*)

The West Window. (© *Bernadette Fallon*)

carved in the early 16th century and pre-dates the *Book of Common Prayer*. The base was added in the 19th century, carved from stone and featuring Christian symbols including the four evangelists. Here you'll find Mark's lion, Luke's ox, John's eagle and the winged man of Matthew.

Curious facts: Mary Magdalene and William Morris

The windows of the cathedral deserve attention. There's a particularly
fine example of an early William Morris work, designed by Morris
and pre-Raphaelite colleagues Ford Madox-Brown, Edward Burne-

Morris window. (© *Bernadette Fallon*)

Jones, Dante Gabriel Rossetti, Peter Marshall and Philip Webb. This was one of their earliest commissions and was originally installed as a single seven-light window in 1863. In the 1950s, it was re-ordered for the cathedral extension as three separate windows, a mammoth jigsaw puzzle involving 30,000 pieces of glass and a lot of very precise planning.

You'll find the majority of this glass in the East Window in the Lady Chapel now, with its large cast of characters including prophets, patriarchs, evangelists, angels and women. One of the women is Mary Magdalene and historical records show that the 'first draft' of Mary Magdalene was returned by the church authorities to Morris and his colleagues. Apparently, the design was deemed 'unsuitably clothed'. We'll never know what she looked like, unfortunately, as the follow-up was deemed more appropriate and duly accepted.

Women once again are a feature in the windows in the south wall, outside the Lady Chapel. These windows depict three strong women, honoured for their work in spreading the Christian faith. Elizabeth was a princess of Hungary in the 13th century who became an early Franciscan, caring for the poor and sick, but was persecuted for her work.

The story of Ethelburga of Kent is told in many cathedrals throughout the north of England, as she was among those responsible for bringing Christianity to the region, encouraging her husband, King Edwin of Northumbria, to convert to the faith, which resulted in many of his subjects following his example. She was a powerful woman, and a friend of the pope's.

Hilda of Whitby was brought up in Ethelburga's household and became Abbess of Hartlepoool, founding a monastery at Whitby that produced five bishops. She battled with Wilfrid, founder of Ripon Cathedral, at the Synod of 664, called to debate if the church should continue to follow the traditional Celtic calendar, established by the Irish monks, or adopt the new Roman one. She argued for tradition, the Synod ruled for Rome.

But the cathedral is not all about ancient history. Bradford celebrates contemporary culture and innovation alongside the tributes it pays to its past and was the first cathedral in the country to generate its own power when it installed forty-two solar panels on the roof in 2011.

The north transept is often used for art exhibitions and other events, and the Bradford City Football Ground Fire Disaster memorial here commemorates that devastating tragedy of 1985. And, in fact, the tremendous efforts of many in the city led to innovations in the treatment of burns and in disaster relief across the world.

Nearby, in the north ambulatory, there are some interesting examples of old meeting new. Worn steps that once led up to the rood loft can be seen within the wall to the left of the window, now tailing off, leading nowhere. The ancient rood loft was removed and the stairs blocked up during the Reformation. This act even had its own 'order', the Order of the Destruction of Rood Lofts.

Don't miss: the Anglo-Saxon cross

Look closely at the wall near the stairs to see an Anglo-Saxon cross fragment, discovered in the rubble of the south nave wall during renovation work in the 19th century. It's believed that the earliest church on the site was built from wood or wattle with a stone cross outside. This cross could even date back to Christianity's supposed arrival in Bradford, when Bishop Paulinus travelled from Kent to the court of King Edwin of Northumbria in the 7th century. You'll see another example of old meets new close to the First World War memorial by the north door, where the digital display shows the output of the solar panels!

Another discovery was made when the old chancel was demolished in 1958, a Medieval piscina, used for the washing of Holy Communion vessels. It now has a small stone inset that came from the Garden of Gethsemane.

Medieval pisina. (© *Bernadette Fallon*)

Don't miss: the 'top-secret' Listers

The Listers were a prominent family in the creation of Bradford's industry and subsequent wealth and are honoured accordingly in the cathedral. Visible from the cathedral, Lister's Mill chimney has been a Bradford landmark since 1873. Standing 250 feet high, the story goes that Samuel Lister climbed to the top to toast it with champagne on completion.

The Listers were world leaders in fabric production, including luxury fabrics like velvets and silks, and they made over 1,000 yards of velvet drapes for the coronation of George V in Westminster Abbey in 1901. During the Second World War, they developed top-secret fabrics for the war effort, including parachute silk, flame-proof woollen cloth and camouflage material. In 1891, they were using 50,000 tons of coal a year. In the 1930s, 7,000 people were still working there. The mill covered 17 acres on several floors, providing around 27 acres of floor space for workers. Today it is part of Bradford's regeneration project, converted into homes, offices, shops and leisure spaces.

It's heart-wrenching to see the number of memorial tablets for children, both inside and outside the building. In the small area around the walls of the tower alone there are forty-five children mentioned. In the graveyard outside there's a stone commemorating a couple and their eighteen un-named infant children.

Bradford's high infant mortality rates were due to pollution and the insanitary conditions of the town. The Hailstone memorial remembers three children out of a family of eight who died – two in the same week. The Hailstones were a prominent local family in the 19th century and lived at Horton Hall.

Don't miss: St Aidan's Chapel

We've met St Aidan in an earlier chapter. He is the 7th-century Irish monk who is acclaimed for bringing Christianity back to Northumbria. He founded a monastic cathedral on the island of Lindisfarne and served as its first bishop, a 'roving bishop' who travelled around the countryside to preach the gospel.

In this chapel you'll find the beautiful carved cross of St Aidan, depicting the needs of both the developing world and the industrial one, reflected in the cathedral's links with its twinned dioceses of Khartoum and South-western Virginia.

Curious facts: the green man in the wood

The carved wooden pulpit is decorated with figures of Matthew, Mark, Luke and John, the gospel writers. But look closely and just below the woodwork you'll see a surprising little face peeping out of the stone leaves – a tiny green man, a link back to Pagan times and a symbol of nature. It's a reminder that for all Bradford's industrialisation and commerce, for all the hustle and bustle of the city streets outside, this church was once known as t'kirk in t'wood – the church in the wood.

Visiting the cathedral

For opening times and more information visit Bradfordcathedral.org.

Bradford: where to go and what to do

It's come a long way since its industrialised past, but part of the charm of this new cosmopolitan city is the interesting way it has incorporated that heritage into its modern fabric. Subject to racial tensions and unrest in past decades, today its multi-cultural community has created a re-invigorated energy – and a huge variety of places to eat excellent curry. The city has been crowned Curry Capital of Britain on several occasions. Experience its cultural influences in one lively blast at the Bradford Festival during the summer, a celebration of Asian food, music, dance, art and culture.

A must-see in the city is the National Media Museum, an eye-catching glass building in the bustling City Park. Have a look at the Mirror Pool as you pass through – though in fairness it would be hard to miss it. It's the largest water feature in the UK with 100 fountains, laser lights and millions of different water effects.

The museum tells the story of media in all of its forms – from film, TV and radio to photography, animation, digital technology, advertising and, of course, the internet. There's plenty to get involved in – like broadcasting your own news bulletin or having a go at some retro video games. Here you'll also find the world's earliest known surviving negative, the earliest television footage and the camera that made the earliest moving pictures in Britain. The museum also houses an IMAX cinema. Bradford is in fact the world's first UNESCO City of Film, recognising the city's rich film heritage and popularity as a movie location.

Experience Bradford's mix of culture in a stroll around the city, from the ubiquitous curry restaurants to the cultural quarters. Head for Little Germany to see what was the world centre for the wool trade, with its stunning collection of 19th-century buildings, fifty-five of which are listed. The area gets its name from the German merchants who developed it from 1860, bringing people from all over the world to work here. Here the wealth from the city's industrial past is most evident. Watch out for Grandad's Clock and Chair on Chapel Street, an interpretation of a mill owners' office with chair, mirror and grandfather clock.

Continue your historical tour at the Wool Exchange in Market Street, the original 19th-century wool trading centre and still a commercial centre today – though now it's used for selling books, housing a Waterstone's shop and café. Created in the Venetian Gothic style, the striking façade features carved portraits of luminaries including Colombus and Francis Drake. Inside, the high ceilings and marble columns display Bradford's historic wealth and grandeur and are an impressive backdrop to a book-browse.

You'll find more wool-related history at Moorside Mills in Eccleshill, built in 1875 as a small spinning mill, now a museum with displays of textile machinery, steam power, engineering and motor vehicles. See how the other half lived in the splendour of the Mill Owner's House, or come down to earth at the Mill Workers' Terraces.

There's more grandeur on offer at Bolling Hall on the outskirts of the city. Take a peek into the lives of the wealthy families who lived here for over 500 years. Parts of the building date back to Medieval times and the rooms are decorated in different periods to create an engaging trip through history. Apparently the Ghost Room is haunted, well the clue is in the name really. Watch out for its White Lady.

For art exhibitions, including a fine collection of international contemporary prints and modern South Asian art and crafts, head to Cartwright Hall, set in the grounds of Lister Park, the home of the famous Bradford industrialists. Here you'll also find the first Mughal Water Garden to be built in the north of England, following the architectural style of the features developed by India's Mughal dynasty. It's a stunning display of terraces, paths, lawns and tree-lined avenues, divided by water channels, cascades and pools.

Check out Bradford's lively social scene. You'll find a big selection of places to eat and drink around the city's newly developed Broadway shopping centre. A crop of quirky independent bars and eateries has popped up in the stylish North Parade area, you'll also find some interesting shops to browse here. Bradford's West End is another area of Bradford undergoing resurgence, with several new bars and restaurants.

Staying in the city? If you're travelling by train you won't find anything more convenient than the Midland Hotel, a throw-back to the days of glamorous railway hotels. Dating from 1885, it retains many of its Victorian features with a grand foyer, glittering chandeliers and an old-world style that befits its location on the edge of the wealthy Little Germany. It's played host to the great and the good of Bradford and the world, including Laurel and Hardy, the Beatles and several UK prime ministers. The Shakespearean actor Sir Henry Irving died on the main staircase, following his performance at the nearby Theatre Royal. He was attended to by his manager Bram Stoker, the author of *Dracula*.

Bradford's close proximity to its larger neighbour Leeds means the two cities have virtually joined up and so it's easy to explore both by car, train or bus. The city is also served by Leeds-Bradford Airport, with domestic and international flights.

Chapter 7

Edinburgh

Revolts, reconciliations and a royal order: St Giles Cathedral, Edinburgh

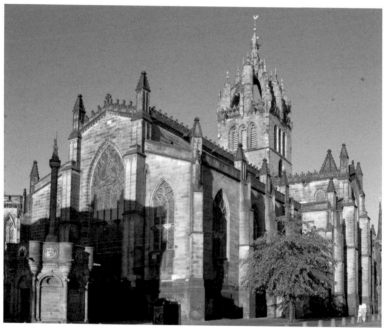

Edinburgh Cathedral. (© *Peter Backhouse: reproduced by kind permission*)

A place of worship for nearly 900 years, St Giles Cathedral has played a tumultuous part in Scottish history and has been a legendary scene of revolts and reconciliations. Today, as well as being Edinburgh's chief seat of worship and a spiritual centre for the community, it holds a special place within its walls for royalty. And dogs.

St Giles was a Greek prince, born in Athens around 650, but he turned his back on worldly pleasures and moved to France to become a hermit in the forests around Nimes. A female deer was his only companion but one day, while the king of the Visigoths was hunting in the forest, Giles was injured protecting the deer from the king's arrow. To apologise, the king built him a monastery. It became a place of pilgrimage and after Giles' death he was associated with many miracles. Today St Giles is the patron saint of woodland, lepers, beggars, cripples and those struck by sudden misery.

It's believed that the church of St Giles was founded around 1124, when King David came to power in Scotland. His elder sister Matilda was known for her work helping lepers and King David granted responsibility for the church to the religious order of the Lazarites, whose chief purpose was to provide care for lepers. It's likely that this is how the church received its name.

Curious facts: the missing bone

Up until the time of the Reformation, a part of St Giles himself reportedly lived in the cathedral: his arm bone, brought back from France in 1454 by Sir William Preston of Gorton. Relics were important in the Middle Ages because relics attracted people and more people meant more money. But the bone disappeared during the plunders of the Reformation and today its location is a mystery.

The Preston aisle was built around 1460 to house the relic and though that particular treasure is gone for good, there are some other interesting ancient artefacts here, including a knight's grave marker from around 1200, a 15th-century headstone and one of the earliest stone carvings of the Edinburgh arms, probably also from the 15th century.

Uncovering the Medieval church of St Giles

Not much is left – or in fact known – of the original church of St Giles, though you can still see a few of its stones, including the top of a small pillar and several grotesque faces, set into the wall at the back of the cathedral. Outside there's some late Medieval stonework on the tower, but everything else was covered by new sandstone when the building was restored in the 19th century.

The sanctuary at the crossing is believed to be the oldest part of St Giles Cathedral, along with parts of the chancel and the south transept, and the four pillars here date from the early 14th century. Looking at the shape of the building from this vantage point, a link with its namesake is also evident. The outline of St Giles resembles a Greek cross, which has a square shape, rather than a Latin one, which is more elongated. So the place where the nave and transepts meet is the centre of the building, rather than closer to the east wall as is common in most churches. The decision to place the holy table here, which is used in St Giles Cathedral in place of an altar, means the minister is surrounded by his congregation during mass, rather than looking out at them from an altar at the back of the church.

There's an interesting piece of history in the chancel ceiling. The boss above the painting of the coat of arms of George II dates back to the original Romanesque church of the early 12th century, making it 200 years older than the other bosses here. And though the Virgin Mary was downgraded from her elevated status in the church after the Reformation, her prime position is still in evidence on the ceiling. Two bosses are inscribed with IHS – the first three letters of the Greek name of Jesus – and with the beginning of the Ave Maria prayer to Mary.

Curious facts: the oldest aisle and a guilty secret

The Albany aisle in the north-west corner is one of the oldest aisles in the building, dating from the early 1400s. The story behind its original creation is not fully known but there are a number of theories. It's known to take its name from the Duke of Albany, a brother to King Robert III and great-grandson of Robert the Bruce. An influential member of a powerful dynasty, he took a special interest in the church of St Giles.

His brother the king was a weak ruler and a frail man and his son David was appointed as lieutenant of the kingdom, under the guidance of the duke. But David was headstrong and failed to follow advice, so Albany imprisoned him. David died at Albany's Palace and while suspicion fell on the duke, he was never found guilty of the death. But many believed the Albany aisle was built out of remorse for the crime.

Don't miss: the chapel of an ancient royal order

St Giles Cathedral's links with royalty continue to the present day. Members of the British royal family are regular visitors to the cathedral because of their connection with the Thistle Chapel, the spiritual home and meeting place of The Most Ancient and Most Noble Order of the Thistle. James VII of Scotland, who was also James II of England, founded it in 1687, though the order may be even older than this and potentially has links back to the early 8th century.

There are sixteen knights and ladies of the Thistle, all appointed by the sovereign, usually to reward achievements in public service, politics, the law and the arts. Currently there are four royal members as well as the queen: the Duke of Edinburgh; Prince Charles, who is known as The Duke of Rothesay in Scotland; Princess Anne; and the Duke of Cambridge. Traditionally the non-royal knights were members of the noble and landowning families of Scotland, but in recent times, appointments have been made from the wider community, including in 1996 the first non-royal lady of the Thistle, music teacher Marion Fraser.

The order has been meeting in St Giles' Thistle Chapel since 1911, and the chapel, despite its High Gothic style, is the newest part of the cathedral. It's made entirely of Scottish materials, including a

Thistle chapel.
(© *Bernadette
Fallon*)

floor of Ailsa Craig granite, inset with pieces of Iona marble, which gives it a link to one of the oldest and most important Christian sites in Scotland, the place from where Christianity spread. The wood is Scottish oak and the stone is from Fife.

The decoration in the chapel is beautifully detailed: dogs and beavers, wild boars and even an elephant and a lion are carved on the armrests between the stalls. Talbot hounds intertwine on the south-west turn of the stalls where the corners meet, wooden panels on the wall are created to resemble folding linen and brass angels hold lights to illuminate the magnificent setting.

Curious facts: St Giles Cathedral and the dogs

So much for royalty and the nobility, what about the dogs? This tradition stretches back to the time of St Giles Cathedral's most famous minister, John Knox. Ordained a Catholic priest in the

John Knox statue. (© *Bernadette Fallon*)

16th century, he converted to Protestantism after meeting George Wishart, an early Protestant reformer, around 1544.

It was a dangerous time to speak out against Catholicism. Wishart was burned at the stake for heresy in 1546 and Knox was taken prisoner and put in a French slave-galley. After rowing for nineteen months, he was set free in France and travelled to the north of England, which was safe for him now that King Henry VIII had cut ties with Rome. But when Queen Mary came to the throne, she restored Catholicism and so Knox was forced out again, going to Europe and teaching in Geneva and Frankfurt.

But by 1559, the reformed faith was becoming increasingly popular in Scotland, and Knox was able to return to his home country. He became the leading preacher in the Reformation and a week after preaching in St Giles' for the first time, he was elected minister, staying in the office for thirteen years. Scotland became officially

John Knox burial plaque. (© *Bernadette Fallon*)

Protestant as parliament passed acts to abolish papal authority and reform the Scottish church in 1560.

And the dogs?

John Knox had a very good friend called John Craig. Travelling on the continent, Craig became very ill and was close to death. His life was saved by a dog, though there is some confusion as to how exactly. But the outcome was that Craig made it back to Scotland, told the story to John Knox who promptly allowed dogs the freedom of the church, and today they are still welcome within the cathedral.

You can visit the site of John Knox's grave in the very inauspicious surroundings of the car park outside. It's not known exactly where he is buried but a plaque on the ground beside bay 23 marks the approximate place.

Wars, unrest and riots in the cathedral

By the time Knox died in 1572, Scotland was a Calvinist country. But things remained extremely unsettled following the Reformation, particularly when Charles 1 came to power in England and Scotland in 1625 and tried to introduce further reform. By now St Giles' was the seat of a bishop and therefore a cathedral, making Edinburgh a city. In 1637, Charles insisted on introducing the *Book of Common Prayer* to the church, following the content of the Anglican prayer book. This caused such dissent when it was used for the first time on 23 July that, legend has it, a woman called Jenny Geddes picked up her stool and threw it at the dean as soon as he started reading from it.

While this event triggered incidents that led to the Bishops' Wars in Scotland and ultimately the Civil War, there is, in fact, no evidence in the cathedral records that a woman called Jenny Geddes actually existed in Edinburgh at the time. There is, however, a 'Janet Geddes' listed among the parishioners a few decades later. So who was this – clearly very annoyed – woman? It has been suggested that 'she' was likely to have been a man dressed as a woman to escape penalty, and was in fact planted in the congregation to instigate a riot that led eventually to the overthrow of the British monarchy.

Emotions intensified in 1638 when the National Covenant was signed, opposing King Charles' involvement in church matters and denying him as head of the Scottish church. The covenant was supported by local notables including the Marquis of Montrose and the Marquis of Argyll, though they were not to unite on the same side for long.

Charles I was executed in 1649 at the climax of the Civil War and Oliver Cromwell arrived in Scotland in 1650. Although he had signed the covenant, Montrose could not condone the killing of the king and was executed as a Royalist in 1650. But when monarchy was restored and Charles II came to the throne in 1660, it was Argyll's turn for the chop. Arrested by the order of the king, he was tried for high treason and executed in 1661 for his collaboration with Cromwell's government.

Montrose's reputation was restored, as were his body parts. His arms and legs had been sent out to Stirling, Glasgow, Perth and Aberdeen as a warning after his execution and were now re-assembled and given a magnificent funeral in St Giles Cathedral. Meanwhile, Argyll's head was placed on the same spike on the city's Tolbooth building where Montrose's had been displayed for over ten years.

Today you can visit memorials for both men in the cathedral, finally reconciled under the same roof in the 19th century. You may find Montrose's monument bedecked with flowers from visitors who come to pay tribute to him, and on a bright day you will find it covered in a beautiful pattern of reds, yellows and oranges from the window installed in the aisle to remember his followers.

The Tolbooth, which housed the early parliaments and also the prison, as well as the head of the Marquis of Montrose post-execution, was demolished in the early 19th century to create more space on the Royal Mile. This threw up a whole new set of problems for St Giles'.

Candles. (© *Bernadette Fallon*)

It became clear that the cathedral walls were leaning outwards and close to collapse. The restoration that took place to solve the problem may have destroyed much of the building's Medieval fabric, but at least it ensured it's still standing.

Don't miss: the writers of Scotland

Around the cathedral you will find many tributes to the great writers of Scotland, often dedicated by celebrities even more famous than those they paid tribute to. In the Moray aisle, you'll find the carved head of Robert Fergusson, an Edinburgh poet who published his

Robert L. Stevenson. (© *Bernadette Fallon*)

collected works in 1771 but died in an asylum just two years later after falling down a flight of steps. He was 24 years old. His great admirer Robert Burns paid for his headstone.

Here too is a plaque to the 19th-century Scottish novelist Margaret Oliphant, which was unveiled by her friend and Peter Pan creator

J.M. Barrie. And the bronze memorial to Robert Louis Stevenson is unusual for bringing smoking into the cathedral. The famous 19th-century Scottish author of *Treasure Island* is shown with a newspaper and a cigarette.

One of the most eye-catching memorials in the cathedral is the Robert Burns window on the west wall, commemorating the 18th-century poet. You can see his figure in the lower centre section, with his signature – taken from one of his last letters – beneath it.

Thee rather startlingly but aptly named Holy Blood aisle holds a tribute to the Earl of Moray James Stewart. Here a window depicts his bloody assassination in 1570, with the mighty John Knox preaching at his funeral. And in fact the earl is buried right here, at the foot of the steps. Moray was a half-brother to Mary, Queen of Scots, and one of her advisers until he became her opponent.

Following her abdication, he became the first of a number of regents ruling Scotland for the infant King James, but was killed by one of Mary's followers in her birthplace, Linlithgow, shot with a gun from a window as he rode down the street. It's believed to be history's first recorded assassination with a gun and the window shows it still smoking as the earl falls from his horse. Look for the detail in the window that shows the interior of St Giles Cathedral as it was in John Knox's time.

Don't miss: the 'secret' in the window

You'll find another interesting story in the window depicting the Last Supper on the east wall. See Judas Iscariot, the hooded figure, creeping out of the room? Up until a few years ago nobody knew he was there. He was only discovered when the windows were cleaned as part of the renewal of St Giles'.

The window next to this, showing Christ's entry into Jerusalem, is dedicated to the memory of Robert Stevenson, whose grandson, Robert Louis Stevenson, is commemorated elsewhere in the building. He was a civil engineer who designed twenty-three Scottish lighthouses, the most famous one situated on the Bell Rock off Arbroath on the east coast of Scotland, the world's oldest surviving lighthouse.

Arbroath is famous for another reason of course. The Declaration of Arbroath is the most famous document in Scottish history and the American Declaration of Independence is believed to be partly based on it. Drafted in Arbroath Abbey on behalf of the nobles of Scotland, it pleads for Scottish independence. A cause that also has been fought out in many ways within the walls of St Giles Cathedral.

Visiting the cathedral

Guided tours of the building run regularly in summer, less frequently in winter. For more information and opening times visit Stgilescathedral.org.uk.

Edinburgh: where to go and what to do

It's an exciting city, vibrant and buzzing with a great cultural scene, lively social life and centuries of fascinating history. But it's not so big as to appear off-putting and lots of the main sights are easily accessible by walking. The buildings are imposing and the views quite amazing from the hilly twists and turns of the old streets. And it's on the sea, just a short bus or train ride from the city centre.

It's fair to say, however, that most guests don't come for the seaside. The home of the world-famous Edinburgh Festival, every August the city is full to bursting with performers and audiences from all over the world. Plan to book your accommodation well ahead if you want to experience the multitude of cultural delights with literally thousands of theatre and comedy shows, exhibitions, gigs, films, readings, talks and much more taking place throughout the month.

It's not the only festival that takes place in the city of course – and it's not even one festival! It includes the Festival Fringe, the International Festival, the Military Tattoo and the International Book Festival. There are plenty of other events taking place throughout the year and you might find them a little quieter.

A good place to start your visit to Edinburgh is on the Royal Mile, well placed for St Giles Cathedral and the city's historic past. Here you'll find the Princes Street Gardens, Edinburgh Castle, the Scottish Parliament, the house of John Knox – after meeting his statue in the cathedral – and the Palace of Holyroodhouse, among other attractions. You won't get through it all in a day and you'll also want to leave time to explore the winding side alleys and shops as you go. But it's a great place to start your city exploration. And make sure you make the climb to Arthur's Seat in the evening for a stunning sunset.

But why is it called the Royal Mile? It got the nickname in the 16th century when it was used by the king to travel between the castle and the Palace of Holyroodhouse. The castle was a royal residence from the 11th century, then served as the British army's main base in Scotland for several centuries before becoming a very famous tourist attraction today. It's well worth a visit. Allow around two hours to do the complete tour.

The Palace of Holyroodhouse is the Royal Family's official residence in Scotland. One of its most famous residents was Mary, Queen of Scots. You can still visit her bedchamber, where she spent the years from 1561 to 1567. In the room next door you'll find a plaque marking the spot where her secretary and friend bled to death, after being killed by Mary's first husband. The palace was originally a guesthouse attached to Holyrood Abbey and the oldest surviving part of the building dates from the early 1500s. The ruined abbey is still visible in the grounds.

The National Museum of Scotland will take you through the city's often turbulent history and is also interesting for its architecture, a blend of Victorian and modern. At the other end of the Royal Mile, the Scottish Parliament was opened by Queen Elizabeth II in 2005 and the public gallery is open to visitors.

And once you've perused the spiritual treasures of St Giles Cathedral, don't forget to check out the mystical Rosslyn Chapel, which has become a magnet for tourists ever since a man called Dan Brown wrote a book called *The Da Vinci Code* that subsequently became a blockbuster film. The chapel features at the end of the story, chosen no doubt for its alleged links to the Knights Templar and the Freemasons.

It was built in the 15th century for William St Clair, the 3rd Earl of Orkney, and it's speculated that the Rosslyn is a secret Templar holding for all sorts of treasures, including the Holy Grail, the head of John the Baptist and even the body of Jesus Christ himself. You'll need to take a short bus ride to the chapel as it's seven miles south of the centre.

For less mystical pursuits, you could visit Edinburgh Zoo, one of the world's leading conservation zoos that has helped save many endangered species including Siberian tigers and red pandas. Princes Street near the Royal Mile is the main place for shopping, though you'll find plenty of tourist shops selling tartan, haggis and woolly jumpers along the Mile itself.

There are a few very grand and historical hotels close to the city centre if you're treating yourself to a luxury visit. The Scotsman Hotel, close to the main railway station, is housed in the former newspaper offices and very plush, while the Balmoral could easily play host to a queen. For something more modest, with a link to religion and the benefit of sea air, the Best Western Kings Manor hotel is housed in a former convent, and walking distance from the beach, east of the city. And yes, it does serve haggis for breakfast.

The city is very well connected to the rest of Scotland and the UK by bus, train and an international airport.

Chapter 8

Aberdeen

Where William Wallace rests – maybe: St Machar's Cathedral, Aberdeen

Aberdeen Cathedral. (© *St Machar's Aberdeen: reproduced by kind permission*)

It had an auspicious beginning but has also been the site of much destruction and dispute, attacked by wars, the Reformation and the weather. It's thought to be the final resting place for Scotland's famous hero William Wallace. Well, part of him at least. It's said that in 1305 the left quarter of his body was brought to Aberdeen after his grisly execution in London by Edward I and interred within the wall of the new cathedral.

More properly known as The Cathedral Church of St Machar, it has played a part in the fight for Scottish independence in conflicts that raged throughout the Middle Ages. This conflict goes deep into the very foundation of the church itself. And has created one of the cathedral's most controversial situations. As we will see.

Who was St Machar?

Today St Machar's is a Presbyterian church that has its origins in the country's Celtic past. St Machar was a Celtic saint and, in his life, a follower of St Columba, an Irish monk who played an important part in spreading Christianity throughout Ireland and what is today Scotland. Machar established a place of worship in Old Aberdeen around 580.

There's good evidence that this 6th-century place of worship was on the site of today's cathedral. In 1131, King David I of Scotland moved a bishopric – the district under a bishop's control – from Mortlach to the cathedral's current site in Aberdeen because of its links with St Machar's church. We know that by 1165, a cathedral in the Norman style had largely been completed on this site

Legend also has it that God told Machar – or Columba, it's not clear who exactly got the message – to build a church where a river bends into the shape of a bishop's crosier. The River Don bends in this way just below where the cathedral now stands.

Like so many cathedrals throughout the UK, the Norman building began to be replaced with one in the Early English style from about 1290. This work was carried out under a number of what have come to be known as 'builder bishops', starting with Bishop Henry de Cheyne. And after William Wallace (or one quarter of him) came back to rest here, the almost-finished cathedral was badly damaged in 1336 when Aberdeen was attacked by Edward III of England. Work still continued, however, and it's thought the building was complete by 1450.

In the 14th century, Bishop Alexander de Kininmund built the fortified west towers and began work on the current nave. He also carried the famous 'Declaration of Arbroath' to the pope. This declaration is still seen by many as the foundation of the Scottish state:

For, as long as but a hundred of us remain alive, never will we on any conditions be brought under English rule. It is in truth not for glory, nor riches, nor honours that we are fighting, but for freedom – for that alone, which no honest man gives up but with life itself.

It pleads for leniency after the pope had excommunicated Robert the Bruce, his followers and his bishops – effectively excommunicating Scotland – during the fight for independence from English rule.

The following century, Bishop Lichtoun completed this nave and began construction of the central tower, while Bishop Elphinstone

The nave. (© *St Machar's Aberdeen: reproduced by kind permission*)

finished the tower and south transept. The century after, between 1518 and 1532, Bishop Dunbar, who was also Chancellor of Scotland, commissioned the Renaissance heraldic ceiling depicting the sovereigns of Europe and the noble and religious families of Scotland. He also added the twin spires at the west front of the cathedral.

The change in St Machar's

Which was all complete just in time for the destruction of the Reformation in the mid-1500s. Statues, relics, documents and all manner of treasures were destroyed in the attempt to remove all traces of 'popery' from the cathedral. St Machar's lost many of its valuable possessions and books, which were stolen or destroyed. The building also lost its cathedral status and became the parish church of Oldmachar. The twenty-nine canons who made up the clergy were forced out and replaced by just two ministers. Now St Machar's was a Presbyterian church, rejecting the elaborate ostentation of the old Catholic faith.

Curious facts: the central tower

In 1654, Cromwell's forces came to Aberdeen and dismantled the church quire to build a fort in the town. This weakened the building's structure and in 1688 the church's central tower fell down during a storm. The transepts and crossing were destroyed, the nave was damaged and its east end bricked up. Centuries would pass until its eventual restoration in 1953. But you can still see the stones of the central tower – if you know where to look. When the tower fell down the masonry was used for building work around Old Aberdeen.

Memorials to some of the builder bishops can be seen throughout the church. A 15th-century effigy of Bishop Henry Lichtoun stands in the west end of the cathedral, nearby you'll find a portrait of Bishop Gavin Dunbar. The Builder Bishops' Window by Douglas

Builder Bishops Window. (© *St Machar's Aberdeen: reproduced by kind permission*)

Strachan dates from 1913 and depicts, from left to right, Bishop Kininmund II, Bishop Elphinstone and Bishop Lichtoun.

Of all the bishops, one of the finest legacies was left by Bishop Dunbar – the magnificent heraldic ceiling erected in 1520. It's a stunning piece of work but not only that, it shows us a very interesting picture of 16th-century Scotland, England and Europe. The rumblings of Reformation were starting to have an impact when this ceiling was commissioned and the old order was on the brink of disintegration.

There are forty-eight shields on the ceiling, including the coats of arms of Scotland's bishops and archbishops, as well as Europe's royal houses, such as the Holy Roman Emperor Charles V, King Henry VIII and the kings of Scotland. Watch out for the politics at play. At the time, Scotland was closely aligned with France in the fight against their common enemy, England. And so the fleur-de-lys arms of France is given higher prominence than the shield of King Henry of England. Notice also that the fleur-de-lys symbol has been left off the English monarch's coat, even though he liked to display it to show his claim to the French throne. The Scottish representation simply ignores it.

The European kingdoms on show represent the important countries of the day, a very different Europe to the one we know now. So while we do have France, Spain and Denmark, we also have Poland, Cyprus, Sicily and Hungary. And Aberdeen asserts its place in this list, making up the final shield in the north row, showing the Burgh of Old Aberdeen, a vase of lilies faced with three intertwined salmon.

If the scarlet lion surrounded by fleur-de-lys on a yellow background – the Royal Scottish Standard – looks familiar to you, you might just have seen it at a football match. It's the personal banner of the Scottish monarch, now the Queen of England. Even though its use is restricted under the Act of Parliament of Scotland 1672, fans have yet to be prosecuted for flying it.

There is only one woman represented on the ceiling. but it's not the Scottish ruler of the time, Margaret Tudor. She was ruling as regent for her son James, who was just 8 years old. The sister of Henry VIII and a very unpopular woman, there was no question of her appearing on the ceiling. Instead that honour goes to St Margaret, wife of King Malcolm Canmore who ruled in the 11th century and was much loved by the Scots.

Curious facts: the pope in the ceiling

Ironically, this Presbyterian congregation, which has no ties to the church in Rome, worships under the arms of the pope every day. Because there at the head of the centre row of shields is the coat of arms of Giovanni de'Medici, Pope Leo X: five red balls with one blue ball bearing the fleur-de-lys of France, all surmounted by the papal crown and pierced by the gold and silver keys of St Peter.

Unlike many of the grand and elaborate cathedrals you will find throughout the country, St Machar's interior is very simple. It is not without its treasures, of course and there are many beautiful details to hold the attention. And the layout you see in St Machar's today would be largely familiar to its 17th-century congregation – who would probably be very interested to see the new east end with its three stained-glass windows.

Don't miss: the Sanctuary Cross

One of the most interesting church treasures is the Sanctuary Cross, whose origins go right back to the early days of the cathedral and beyond, to its Celtic associations with Machar himself.

In 1919, the top of a stone Celtic cross was discovered in Old Aberdeen. Research showed it to be the 12th-century cross that had stood in the cathedral grounds, promising to all the protection of the church. Work began to restore it in 2000, under the care of

Sanctuary Cross. (© *St Machar's Aberdeen: reproduced by kind permission*)

local stonemason Alistair Urquhart. It is believed that Aberdeen's Sanctuary Cross was created by the same French stonemason who carved St Helen's Cross at Kelloe in County Durham, and its design provided the inspiration for the restoration.

The original sandstone had to be matched to today's colours, the plinth and shaft had to be carved, the word 'Sanctuary' was etched on the bottom. And finally, erecting a scaffold in the cathedral, the cross was raised into position and its return was complete, many hundred years later.

At the west end of the aisle, above the vestry door, is a Celtic stone cross of the 7th century, which was discovered in a dyke to the east of the church. It was installed in the cathedral in 1997 by the University of Aberdeen to mark the college's 500-year association with the church. The university was founded by one of St Machar's builder bishops, Bishop Elphinstone.

Don't miss... the Barbour Tryptych

In the south aisle, the wooden Barbour Tryptych is dedicated to the 14th-century poet John Barbour, who wrote the epic poem *The Brus* and who was for forty years Archdeacon of Aberdeen. Also known as *The Bruce*, it's a long narrative poem of just under 14,000 lines, written in Early Scots to give an account of the actions of Robert the Bruce in the Scottish Wars of Independence.

Barbour Tryptych. (© *St Machar's Aberdeen: reproduced by kind permission*)

The poem's centrepiece is an account of the Battle of Bannockburn in 1314, which marked an important victory for the Scots in their fight for independence, led by Robert the Bruce. It's considered Barbour's masterpiece and largely regarded to be historically accurate, though it's believed he did exaggerate the numbers of the army. It was written around 1375 to honour the then King of Scotland and Robert the Bruce's grandson, Robert II.

Alongside the effigy of Bishop Lichtoun in the west end of the cathedral are two other very well-preserved late Medieval effigies, which are interesting for the details they show of the contemporary dress of that time. One is unknown, the other is Walter Idyll, a church canon who died in 1468.

You'll need to go outside the cathedral to track down even more of its treasures – to the east of the building, where some of the original walls of the crossing and transepts can be made out, left behind when this part of the building fell down. There's also a tomb that was inside the building before its collapse.

There are many headstones in the churchyard. Graves of note include Bishop Gavin Dunbar and artist Robert Brough, RSA. The Glover family burial ground is also here. Thomas Glover, known as the 'Scottish Samurai', was one of the founders of modern industrial Japan.

Today the cathedral is mighty in its majesty and has been a beacon of spiritual belief through centuries of bloodshed and destruction. But think about this for a minute. The Cathedral Church of St Machar is not a cathedral at all. Or rather, it is one in name only. It was stripped of its cathedral status during the Reformation, like so many other churches. However, while others had their status reinstated, St Machar's, being a Presbyterian church, did not. Technically, St Machar's is no longer a cathedral but rather a High Kirk, as it has not been the seat of a bishop since 1690.

Visiting St Machar's

For information and opening times, visit Stmachar.com.

Aberdeen: where to go and what to do

Located in Aberdeenshire on the east coast of Scotland, this has from Medieval times has been one of the richest and most fertile regions of the Highlands. You may have heard of Aberdeen Angus beef cattle? This is where they come from. And you'll find plenty of places here to sample this local delicacy.

Impressive granite buildings set this city apart, particularly in Old Aberdeen, and taking a walking tour through its history and architecture is highly recommended. There is no sign of 21st-century high streets as you wander around the cobbled lanes of the university quarter in the steps of the Gordons, the Leslies and the Frasers, the founding families of Aberdeen.

The name 'Old Aberdeen' is a bit misleading. It's certainly old but the city area of Castlegate is older still. The name 'Old Aberdeen' came originally from 'Aulton', from the Gaelic term for 'village by the pool'. It's here you'll find St Machar's Cathedral.

While you're in the area, make time to visit the King's Museum, which has an interesting exhibition of 18th-century artefacts from the university – the collection changes regularly. It's housed in the Old Town House, which also has a visitors' centre and tells the story of the local history.

Head for Castlegate to continue your historical tour. This was once the site of public executions and the gallows was located in the Gallowgate, just off the main square. If you want to find the exact spot of the hangings, look out for the bus lane next to the courts. A patch of granite paving in the ground marks the place of the gallows.

Surrounded by beautiful old granite buildings, it can be easy to forget that Aberdeen is a bustling commercial city and an important centre for the North Sea offshore oil industry. Head for the harbour to visit the Aberdeen Maritime Museum and discover that story.

Aberdeen Art Gallery shows contemporary Scottish and English works, alongside historical collections such as the Pre-Raphaelites, housed behind a grand old façade. And you'll find further examples of history meeting modernity at Marischal Colleges, founded in 1593 by the 5th Earl of Marischal and merged in 1860 with King's College, dating from 1495, to create the University of Aberdeen. The building's impressive granite front is the world's second-largest granite structure, after L'Escorial in Madrid, and dates from 1906.

This being Scotland, there is, naturally, plenty of Scotch. The 210-year-old Glen Garioch distillery is just a few miles outside the city. Located in granite buildings that sparkle in the sun, it's been producing single malt since 1797 and you can visit the room where 40,000 tonnes of barley were once turned by hand.

These days the production is mechanised, but links to the workers, who toiled to produce what is now one of the oldest Scotch whiskies in the world, remain in the museum where their photos line the walls. And watch out for 'spirits' of another kind on your visit. According to the tour guides, the old rooms are haunted. At the end of the tour you get to sample the produce. Make sure you try out some of the vintage bottles, malts that have been waiting for up to thirty years to be drunk.

And, with Aberdeen being a coastal city, make time for a trip to the sea and walk the miles of gorgeous seafront promenade. If sailing is more your thing, you can take a cruise around the harbour or venture further out to see dolphins and other wildlife.

For some olde-worlde glamour, the Aberdeen Malmaison Hotel and Spa is a beautiful granite building on the outskirts of the city on a quiet pleasant road. While you're there, try some of the local beef. The Brasserie at the Aberdeen Mal is famous for its steaks.

Aberdeen is well-served by trains and buses, you can also fly to the city's airport from a number of domestic airports.

Glossary

Aisle
A passage running parallel to the nave and usually separated from it by piers, columns or arches

Altar
Table of wood or stone behind which the priest and clergy stand during the order of service and upon which Holy Communion, also known as the Eucharist, is celebrated

Altarpiece
A work of art, often taking the form of separate painted panels that sits above the altar

Anglican church
Part of the Church of England, the reformed church that was established by the English Reformation in the 16th century in opposition to the Roman Catholic church

Apse
A church extension that is usually vaulted and in the shape of a semi-circle

Baptistery
An area containing the font where baptisms take place, either part of the main church or in a separate recess or room

Bishopric
The see, office, diocese or district under a bishop's control

Boss
A richly detailed raised ceiling ornament

Buttress
A structure built to support a wall

Cathedra
The seat or throne of a bishop, from which the world cathedral is derived

Catholic church
Part of the Roman Catholic Church that was founded by Jesus Christ and is headed by the Bishop of Rome, known as the pope

Chancel
The part of the church close to the altar, often enclosed, and reserved for the clergy and church officials

Chantry chapels
Pre-Reformation chapels funded by wealthy individuals or families, where priests were employed to say daily masses for the souls of the departed family members, mainly destroyed during the Reformation. York Minster had as many as sixty chantry chapels by the time of the Reformation in the reign of King Henry VIII

Chapel
A recess or small room within the building for quiet prayer and reflection, usually containing an altar and often dedicated to a saint

Chapter House
The building or room where the cathedral's chapter meets. In Anglican and Catholic canon law a chapter is a college (chapter) of clerics formed to advise a bishop

Choir
A group of singers who mainly perform in church services

Choir (also known as Quire)
The part of the chancel between the sanctuary and nave, that is normally reserved for the choir and church clergy, usually richly decorated

Choir stall
A seat in the choir that is often ornately styled and decorated

Church of England
The English branch of the western Christian church that was established during the 16th-century Reformation by Henry VIII, rejecting the Pope's authority and bringing the church under control of the monarch

Cist burial
A cist is a small stone-built coffin-like box, chest, building, well or site made to serve as the burial place of human remains

Clerestory
The upper level of the nave, transepts and choir, with windows

Cloister
A covered outdoor passageway, usually built against one wall of the building and open on the other side with pillars

Crossing
The part of the building where the nave and transepts meet

Cruciform
A ground plan that is laid out in the shape of a cross

Crypt
The vault underneath a church that is usually reserved for burial and tombs

Decorated Gothic

The second phase of Gothic architecture in the UK, following Early English, where simple shapes gave way to more complex curves, flying buttresses became popular forms of support and decorations on buildings became more detailed

Domesday Book

A survey of all land and property in the kingdom of William the Conqueror following his victory at the Battle of Hastings

Early English architecture

The early period of English Gothic architecture that flourished at the end of the 12th century for 100 years, featuring pointed arches and ribbed vaults, favouring simple lines and fine proportion over elaborate decoration

Episcopalian church

An autonomous branch of the Anglican Church in Scotland, established in the 16th century following the Scottish Reformation

Font

A basin supported on a column where baptisms take place

Green man

This motif is found in many cathedrals around the UK and in cultures around the world. Usually represented as a face surrounded by leaves, its origins are thought to be Pagan, symbolising the spirit of nature and the cycle of growth every spring

Gothic style

A type of architecture popular from the 12th to the 16th century, characterised by pointed rather than rounded arches, rib vaulting and taller slimmer buildings built to create the illusion of soaring up to heaven

Lady Chapel
A chapel in a church that is dedicated to the Virgin Mary

Minster
A minster was the Anglo–Saxon name for a missionary church attached to a monastery. The word is associated with the Latin *monasterium* or monastery. The term dates back to the royal foundation charters of the 7th century, but with the establishment of parish churches from the 11th century, minsters became less common

Misericords
Tip-up seats designed to let clergy rest during prayers. A ledge under the seat gives support to somebody standing when the seat is turned up

Nave
The main body of the cathedral running from the main entrance, which is normally in the west, to the choir. The word comes from the Latin word 'navis', which also gives us the word navy

Norman style
A form of architecture introduced to the UK by William the Conqueror, characterised by round arches, heavy masonry and buildings that are more squat than tall

Orthodox church
With its roots in the church established by Jesus Christ and the apostles, a split occurred in the 11th century causing the Orthodox and Roman Catholic churches to divide. The Orthodox church has its roots in the Eastern Roman Empire, also known as the Byzantine Empire. It doesn't accept the authority of the pope and uses ancient forms of service

Perpendicular style
The final stage of Gothic architecture in the UK, following Early English and Decorated styles, characterised by an emphasis on vertical lines

Piscina
A stone basin

Presbyterian church
Part of the reformed Protestant church, governed by a representative assembly of elders

Protestant church
A member of the western Christian churches that were separated from the Roman Catholic church in the Reformation, including the Baptist, Presbyterian and Lutheran churches

Pulpit
A raised stand or platform where a member of the clergy preaches and delivers sermons

Reredos
The ornamental screen or cloth behind an altar, designed to give the congregation a visual focus as they receive communion

Rood
A crucifix, specifically at the entrance to a chancel

Rood loft
A gallery created to display the rood and its screen

Rood screen
A partition separating the end of the nave from the entrance to the chancel that supports the rood. Also known as a choir screen, chancel screen or jube

Sanctuary
The most sacred part of the church, containing the altar

Sheela-na-gig
A Medieval figure of a naked female with the legs wide apart and the hands emphasising the genitals. The word derives from the Irish *Sile na gcioch*, literally 'Sheila of the breasts', and is thought to be a pre-Christian fertility or mother-goddess symbol

Transept
The passageway either side of the nave, creating the 'arms' of the cross in the cruciform floor plan, usually running north to south with the nave running west to east

Further Reading

A History of Sheffield, David Hey (Carnegie Publishing, 2010)

Aberdeen Memories: A Hidden Archive Uncovered, Raymond Anderson (DB Publishing, 2013)

Aspects of Sheffield, Melvyn Jones (Wharncliffe Books, 1997)

Bloody Scottish History: Aberdeen, Elma Mcmenemy (The History Press, 2014)

Durham Cathedral: A Pilgrimage in Photographs, Philip Nixon & Michael Sadgrove (Amberley Publishing, 2013)

Durham Cathedral: Light of the North, John Field (Third Millennium Publishing, 2006)

Edinburgh: A History of the City, Michael Fry (Pan, 2010)

England's Cathedrals by Train, Murray Naylor (Pen & Sword Books, 2013)

Ripon Cathedral: Its History and Architecture, Bill Forster (Bill Forster and Ian Stalker, 2010)

Ripon Through Time, Maurice Taylor & Alan Stride (Amberley Publishing, 2011)

Secret Bradford (Eyewitness Accounts), Mark Davis (Amberley Publishing, 2014)

St Giles: The Dramatic Story of a Great Church and its People, Rosalind K Marshall (St Andrew Press, 2009)

The Ecclesiastical History of the English People, The Venerable Bede (Courier Corporation, 2012)

The History of England: Tudors, Peter Ackroyd (Pan Macmillan, 2014)

The History of York: From Earliest Times to the Year 2000, Patrick Nuttgens (Blackthorn Press 2007)

The Making of Wakefield 1800–1901, Kate Taylor (Wharncliffe Books, 2008)

The Oxford Illustrated History of the Reformation, Peter Marshall (OUP, 2015)

The Story of Bradford, Alan Hall (The History Press, 2013)

Thomas Wolsey Late Cardinal, His Life and Death, George Cavendish (Rowman & Littlefield, 1974)

Wakefield Cathedral, Kate Taylor & Malcolm Warburton (Jarrold Publishing, 2006)

York Minster: A Living Legacy, Richard Shephard (Third Millennium Publishing, 2008)

Index